The No-Business-Plan
Business Plan

∎

START
ME
UP!

By

EBONG EKA

CAREER
PRESS
Pompton Plains, NJ

START ME UP!
EDITED BY KIRSTEN DALLEY
TYPESET BY EILEEN MUNSON
Cover design by Amanda Kain
Author photo by Moshe Zusman Photography Studio
Printed in the U.S.A.

To order this title, please call toll-free 1-800-CAREER-1 (NJ and Canada: 201-848-0310) to order using VISA or MasterCard, or for further information on books from Career Press.

The Career Press, Inc.
220 West Parkway, Unit 12
Pompton Plains, NJ 07444
www.careerpress.com

Library of Congress Cataloging-in-Publication Data

CIP Data Available Upon Request.

Contents

Foreword 5

Preface 7

Chapter 1: Fears and Doubts 9

Chapter 2: Invention vs. Innovation 27

Chapter 3: Small Business Pitfalls 31

Chapter 4: The Four S's: Structure 37

Chapter 5: Pain Points: Aspirin vs. Vitamin. 41

Chapter 6: Idea Hierarchy Model. 45

Chapter 7: What's Your Niche?. 49

Chapter 8: Become an Expert in Your Niche 53

Chapter 9: The Elevator Pitch. 61

Chapter 10: Entity Structure. 65

Chapter 11: Tax Issues 73

Chapter 12: The Four S's: Strategy (Pricing). 79

Chapter 13: Know Your Numbers 101

Chapter 14: Customer/Market Fit 103

Chapter 15: The Fours S's: Systems (Process). 105

Chapter 16: Virtual Assistants and Interns. 111

Chapter 17: Websites 113

Chapter 18: Raising Money. 127

Chapter 19: The Four S's: Sales 135

Chapter 20: Getting Your First Customer 141

Chapter 21: Content Marketing and Storytelling 147

Chapter 22: Social Media Marketing Tips 155

Chapter 23: Facebook 159

Chapter 24: LinkedIn 167

Chapter 25: YouTube 175

Chapter 26: Twitter 185

Chapter 27: Google+ Techniques 195

Chapter 28: Social Media Tools 203

Chapter 29: Social Media Marketing Techniques 207

Chapter 30: E-mail Marketing 209

Resources 213

Appendix 215

Index 217

About the Author 223

Dedication and Acknowledgments 224

Foreword

If you are like me, you probably spend days and nights wanting to turn your ideas into something that will change the world while making millions of dollars doing it. If you haven't already, you'll quickly learn that hard work and a great idea simply aren't enough to strike it rich. To succeed, you also need a lot of knowledge, support, and a solid plan. Unfortunately, it took me five tries to understand the importance of planning. When I started Clutter Cleaner in 2006, my instinct told me that I should help relocating seniors move, but my planning told me to focus on cleaning out homes effected by hoarding. The business quickly took off, and I eventually became the number-one "extreme cleaner" for the television show *Hoarders*. Years later my company helps families cleaning out hoarded homes, estates, and everything in between. As a result of proper planning, I finally have a successful business helping millions of families worldwide, and I've gained that freedom of working for myself that we all strive for.

I've known Ebong for years as a friend, a fellow entrepreneur, and a mentor. I've personally watched Ebong learn from both the success and failure that a small business can provide. In addition to his experience, passion, and relentless hard work, Ebong has the unique ability to educate others and put his lessons into the framework needed to start a business of your own today. I personally don't believe in spending a year writing a 200-page business plan that becomes too confusing or outdated by the time it's done. The world moves much faster these days, and we need a better and quicker way to start a business. The American Dream is still alive but it's changing quickly, and it's not what your parents or professors thought it was. As a Certified Public Accountant, small business expert, and television personality, Ebong is the perfect person to help you get your idea and dream started.

Running a business that cleans the messiest homes in the world has taught me a few things. Doing the work that no one wants to do is extremely profitable, and proper planning is essential to stay focused throughout your journey towards your first of many successful businesses. Ebong's experience and principals will help make your great ideas and hard work profitable.

—Matt Paxton,
Founder of Clutter Cleaner and
Extreme Featured Cleaner on A&E *Hoarders*

Preface

Business plans are bullshit, and yours probably is, too!

America is the land of opportunity, and entrepreneurship is a symbol of this opportunity that the American Dream is supposed to provide. The essence of the American Dream is taking a new idea and turning it into a successful business. This also happens to be the basic concept of entrepreneurship. In America, the dream of entrepreneurship becomes a reality for many people every day.

With the current unstable economic climate, a growing number of women, minorities, and military veterans are starting businesses to supplement or replace their income. Losing a job can be the perfect opportunity to start a business. According to a 2012 *Huffington Post* article, 15 percent of entrepreneurs launched their own ventures after losing their job. The Kauffman Foundation estimates as much as 543,000 new businesses are started every month.

So how do you start a business? People often say that you need to write a business plan, but what does that mean? You may know a lot about your idea, but not as much about business per se. Know this: starting a business should *not* be about writing a business plan. You're reading this book because you have an idea that you want to capitalize on. More importantly, you have either lost your job or you're tired of working at your current job. The pain of waking up every day and not focusing on your passion continues to grow until that passion turns into regret. Sound familiar? So what's stopping you this time?

Everyone talks about how bad the economy is and how there are no jobs. They are only partially right. The people who are lucky enough to have jobs sit in their cubicles dreaming of a better life. These people have dreams of entrepreneurship and may even start a side gig until they can break free. By definition, a job is not slavery, but for many of you who have a marketable professional skill or a truly different idea, it may as well be. Every day that passes is another day you have not started on the path to your dream.

Whether you want to start a business on the side or jump feet first into your own business, there is a better way to do it. Most businesses fail, but the reality is that most of these failures are preventable. More importantly, your business plan will not help you but will only accelerate your potential failure. The good news is there is no longer a need for a traditional business plan! There is also no longer a need for any start-up confusion because there is a better and more efficient way to start your business. I am going to show you how to start with an idea, charge more money for your services, and get more clients using a better plan for your business—the no-business-plan business plan! Ready? Let's go!

Chapter 1
Fears and Doubts

The list of potential fears, doubts, and excuses that would-be entrepreneurs have to contend with is virtually endless, but the five that I've listed here are probably what most of you are dealing with right now. They are as follows:

1. Starting a business is hard.
2. How do I know if my idea is even worth pursuing?
3. My idea isn't unique.
4. My friends and family think my idea is stupid.
5. I don't have the time to start a business.

Fear #1: Starting a business is hard

The reality is starting a business is easy, but making it last is hard. The key is following the right steps when you start your business. The right steps also apply even if you've already started your business because you will be able to figure out what's missing. People think starting a business is extremely difficult and requires unique skills. As a result, they create barriers to starting one by saying things such as "It takes a lot of luck to be successful." The reality is that luck has little, if anything, to do with it. Anything worth pursuing that is potentially lucrative will be difficult at times. What will get you through those inevitable difficulties are the guidelines that you've already followed in the past.

Many successful people have had to overcome a tremendously difficult experience. Overcoming that difficult experience set the tone for their future success because it was an experience they could draw upon in the event of adversity in the future. Playing professional basketball in Europe required me to overcome some pretty difficult experiences. I played Division III basketball at Calvin College in Grand Rapids, Michigan. If you're familiar with college basketball,

NCAA Division III is the lowest of all divisions and is generally comprised of student athletes who weren't good enough to play at the higher division colleges, such as University of Michigan or Louisville.

I played the starting forward position as a senior in college but only made the "Honorable Mention" All Conference Team. I wasn't on the Conference First or Second Teams, but Honorable Mention—third team, or an afterthought. In addition, I only averaged about 10 points per game, which isn't much for an athlete who wants to play basketball professionally, regardless of the level.

Athletes with my background and experience almost never get the opportunity to play professional sports after college. I had my own list of fears and doubts that should have persuaded me to pursue something else. These fears and doubts were:

- I played at a Division III college.
- I wasn't the best player on my team.
- I didn't have a high scoring average (only 10 points per game).
- I had a limited offensive game; I couldn't score points in a variety of ways.

If I had listened to these fears and doubts, I would never have tried to play professional basketball. Instead, I would have started my accounting career right away. Starting my accounting career right out of college wouldn't have been a bad thing, but I had a dream to play basketball after college. This is what convinced me to go for it:

- I was young and had recently graduated from college.
- The ability to use my mind for accounting had a longer shelf life than my body's shelf life for playing basketball.
- There was little financial risk in attempting to play professional basketball overseas.

Starting a business is a lot easier than playing a professional sport, but both are difficult to accomplish unless you follow the right steps. I created and followed the right steps and ended up playing professional basketball in Europe for two years. Later in this book, I'll share what I did to overcome the odds and be successful.

Fear #2: How do I know if my idea is even worth pursuing?

Starting a business also requires understanding and the ability to evaluate your idea. Not all ideas are worth pursuing; many, quite frankly, stink. The goal is figuring out whether your idea stinks before you sink thousands of dollars into it. You can learn business lessons in one of two ways: with your money, or with someone else's money. You can learn from your mistakes or from the mistakes and wisdom of others, but it's cheaper to learn from the mistakes of others. Several years ago, I learned a business lesson with my own money. Despite the loss and angst, it was still the best crash course in business I ever could have taken.

In 2005 I came up with an idea for a software application that allowed you to create ringtones with your own music. This probably sounds utterly ridiculous now, because iPhone and Android apps are plentiful these days, but eight years ago the idea was cutting edge. I believed in my idea so much that I used a popular online marketplace to find IT resources in India. After several horrible experiences of no communication and false promises, I was burned by the two companies I hired. The venture cost me approximately $10,000 and a lot of aggravation. After licking my wounds, I realized there were deeper lessons to be learned. The major realization was that I had learned this lesson using my own money instead of using someone else's money. It would have been cheaper to take a university course; however, I wouldn't have learned the answer to a very important question: *Who would be willing to pay me money to make a mobile ringtone?* It was a question I had failed to answer before embarking on my outsourcing mission to India. We'll revisit the importance of answering questions like this later in the book.

Fear #3: My idea isn't unique

The idea that an idea must be unique to be good is an annoying (and very common) misconception. When you ask people about their idea for a business or invention, they tend to end their sentence with "...and there's nothing out there like it!" What they don't realize is that this isn't necessarily a good thing.

I recently spoke to a close friend who has an interesting business idea. He has a high-paying job in the Washington, DC area, but he still has that entrepreneurial itch. His idea is to open and run a high-end deli or sandwich shop in his neighborhood, a Washington, DC suburb. I asked him why he felt there needed to be a high-quality deli/sandwich shop in his area. His reply was, "There's nothing really like it and I think it's a hybrid between the high-end and low-end culinary options." As I have so many other times, I replied, "America is about competition, so there's probably a good reason why there aren't any!" As we talked about the idea, we quickly realized that we had a mutual friend who owns several restaurants in the same neighborhood. It made better sense to ask him for some feedback based on his experiences in the restaurant industry and the area.

Our friend said, "The area is fickle. There's another restaurant owner in the area who felt the neighborhood needed a healthy food alternative: salads, wraps, and the like. He opened it and no one came—ever. That experiment lasted about four months before he turned it into a greasy hot dog and sausage shop. People lined up around the block for it!" The good news is my friend wasn't very serious about starting this high-quality deli/sandwich shop. The point here is that the uniqueness of the idea is almost irrelevant to a business taking off.

Uniqueness isn't a prerequisite for a good business; in fact, it probably means your idea is bad! You actually want the opposite of unique—you want an idea that may already exist but requires a slight variation or improvement, such as better service. Being the first to the small-business party is only important in certain industries. Two examples would be pharmaceuticals or the invention of new products. While being first can afford you the ability to patent or protect your invention, that still doesn't mean your business is assured success. Being first only means others can and will copy your idea, learn from your failures, and then go on to create a better product or service. Entrepreneurs who subscribe to that belief tend to fail, while those who come after tend to do a better job than their predecessors.

When I give presentations or speeches, I often ask clients and audience members to tell me what the first popular social network was. Those who know the answer tend to be in their late 30s, while the younger people will say that they've heard of it. Friendster was the first popular social network in the United States. Friendster's problems have been widely discussed. Despite raising a lot of money from venture capitalists, Friendster couldn't overcome two major problems:

1. The Website constantly crashed and took as long as 40 seconds to load due to the large demand of users.

2. Friendster had leadership disagreement on overall strategy. They focused on advertising deals and other product offerings instead of on the fundamental problem of the Website crashing.

MySpace and Facebook were able to surpass Friendster by systematically growing their business. As of this writing, Facebook is the leader, with approximately one billion users worldwide, and it does not appear to be making the same mistakes as its predecessors.

The bigger lesson was understanding how and why Facebook was able to grow. Facebook came after two of the market leaders in social networking and learned from their mistakes. There were three important mistakes that their predecessors made:

1. Friendster: The Website (service) didn't work as advertised and continually crashed when the servers were overloaded.

2. Friendster: The company tried to be all things to all people by providing services that may not have been important to their current users.

3. Myspace: User authenticity and profile consistency were at issue. When I was on Myspace, users were allowed to create custom layouts and backgrounds. In addition, it appeared easier for users to create fake profiles and misrepresent themselves.

This is what Facebook did in response:

■ The company restricted users to certain colleges in a slow and systematic growth approach so as not to overwhelm the Internet servers.

- Facebook focused on what their users cared about: the social interactions of their friends. The company added features later on as the number of users grew.

- Facebook only allows one account per user; creating additional or fake profiles violates its TOS (terms of service). In addition, Facebook proactively deletes fake or questionable profiles as they become available.

Fear #4: My friends and family think my idea is stupid

I love sharing my ideas with people because the chances that my business will take off exponentially increase when others help. Part of that help can include advice, guidance, mentorship, and sometimes even money. Most deals are done through relationships, rarely through solicitation. Who you know is important in the start-up phase of your business. This is why I often tell budding entrepreneurs that worrying about people stealing your ideas is a waste of time. There's actually a lesser chance of you actually starting your business if you keep your idea to yourself. If you can't patent your idea, there's a good chance someone else is already working on starting a business based on that idea anyway.

Many of you are reluctant to share your idea with family and friends because you're afraid of what their reactions will be. During recent travels to the Midwest, I met a talented hotel bartender named Sherie. She was of Filipino descent, born and raised in the United States. She was also a married mother of three. She loved cooking traditional Filipino food, including the popular lumpia, the Filipino version of the egg rolls. She made some lumpia for the hotel's catering manager and staff. Saying the hotel staff loved her lumpia would be an understatement because they couldn't stop raving about how great they were. Sherie then told me her catering manager liked them so much that she wanted to put them on the hotel restaurant's menu. Sherie's excitement of knowing that her colleagues and manager loved her traditional dish grew when she realized that she could start a business around it.

I checked back with Sherie several weeks after our conversation and she still hadn't started her business. When I asked her why, she said, "Well, I spoke to a few friends and family, and they told me that it's too much of an undertaking. They also said that I don't know anything about business and that I'm way over my head with it. I agree with them." Talking yourself out of a business idea is actually a pretty common problem. It is also common for others to try to talk you out of your idea by presenting their fears as valid reasons for not starting a business.

The feedback you receive from friends and family may be valid at times, but more often it is not. Sherie's family was right in that she had no business experience and the project could potentially be a big undertaking. Starting a business is *always* a big undertaking, so that comment was essentially useless. The major difference in Sherie's case was she already had her first customer. She had a customer that wanted to purchase her product before she had even started. The hotel wanted to place a small order to gauge customer interest, after which they could increase the order. The hotel also would have let her prepare the lumpia in its kitchen, which would have saved further costs. She had the ability to slowly build a food business based on her cooking talents.

So what do you do when you receive this kind of feedback from friends and family?

The key to getting your business idea off the ground lies with finding the right advice, guidance, and mentorship from the right people—people who have experience in:

a. the particular industry you're interested in;

b. building businesses similar to yours;

c. developing key relationships that you can use to deal with business pitfalls.

Here's an example. If I'm starting a hamburger stand business, it would be better to ask advice from people in the restaurant industry who built their own hamburger stand or have managed a similar business. I would not ask Donald Trump, Warren Buffett, or some other titan of industry unless that industry were relevant. Family, friends, and strangers will offer their unsolicited opinions on your idea because they have no ideas of their own. Let's face it: the idea of starting a business has already created anxiety for you; the last thing you need is someone with no experience or industry knowledge telling you that your idea sucks! (I will tell you that your idea sucks, too, but I'll also show you how to fix it!) In my case, I minimize business relationships with those who offer useless advice and unfounded opinions. I seek to build relationships with people who've experienced the ups and downs of entrepreneurship. I also seek relationships with people who have experience in the industry I'm interested in because I want to learn more about it.

Fear #5: I don't have the time to start a business

Starting a business requires a lot of effort and resources, time being the most obvious one. Lack of productivity is one of the largest problems small-business owners struggle with. Many of you are starting a business while you still have a full-time job. So you work a nine-hour day and then rush home to your family in time for dinner. By 8 o'clock you're back at the computer again but not to work—to check Facebook, answer e-mails, and basically goof off.

Vilfredo Pareto was an economist famously known for the Pareto Principle, or the 80/20 Rule. He developed the principle after surmising that 80 percent of Italy's wealth was owned by approximately 20 percent of the population. The principle was also applied to other areas of life, including the business world. One example is that 80 percent of a business' revenues come from 20 percent of the owner's or management's efforts. The ancillary application for us is productivity. Dr. Arthur Hafner, Dean of University Libraries at Ball State University, summarized the Pareto Principle's application to productivity as follows:

> To maximize personal productivity, realize that 80 percent of one's time is spent on the trivial many activities. Analyze and identify which activities produce the most value to your company and then shift your focus so that you concentrate on the vital few (20 percent). What do you do with those that are left over? Either delegate them or discontinue doing them. (source: *www.bsu.edu/libraries/ahafner/awh-th-math-pareto.html*)

Productivity is an even bigger problem when you're a small-business owner because your time is extremely limited. The importance of organization and productivity was driven home for me in an interview I conducted with a mother, wife, corporate executive, and serial entrepreneur named Yesi Morillo-Gual.

Yesi Morillo-Gual grew up in the Washington Heights area of New York City as one of five children to immigrant parents from the Dominican Republic. Her father worked 16- to 18-hour days while her mother stayed home with the children. At the age of five, Yesi's world changed when her father died unexpectedly. This tragedy created a tremendous financial burden for her mother, who was now solely responsible for five children in one of the poorest neighborhoods of New York City.

Entrepreneurs aren't born but made through their experiences. Those experiences often serve as the foundation and catalyst for success. Struggle, for example, can be an ingredient for entrepreneurial greatness. At the age of seven, Yesi's first job and entrepreneurial experience occurred at her local supermarket. She witnessed a problem (or "pain point") that her manager was interested in solving. Yesi noticed that at the end of the day there were a lot of "go-backs" at each of the cashier's stations. (Go-backs are shopping items that customers no longer want to buy when they get to the cash register, and therefore they have to go back to the shelves.) The cashiers were responsible for putting these items back, and it sometimes took as long as an hour to return them all. The manager had to pay an extra hour of wages to each cashier for returning items to shelves, which ended up costing as much as $60 each night. Yesi noticed the opportunity and, as she put it, "asked for a raise" by offering to return all the go-backs for $30.

In short, she saw the opportunity, the timing, and the customer benefit and was able to provide a service at a good price. The lesson she learned that day was that, in her own words, "a lot of times in life, you just have to ask for what you want." It's easier to receive what you want if the customer benefits, as well. The same thing goes for your small business. Here's how: *It's easier to charge your customers more money for a service if you can provide added value. Price no longer becomes a topic of conversation, but the value you're adding does.*

Instead of waiting for success and prosperity to find her, this superwoman became a serial entrepreneur by starting notary public, VA (virtual assistant), and networking events planning businesses. The notary public and VA businesses were started in the late 80's and early 90's as a way for Yesi to pay for college. She paid for her bachelors and masters degrees and 80 percent of her doctorate. "I remember those days; I did [the] majority of the course work for my advanced degrees on the train to and from work."

"One of the biggest mistake people make is they wait until they're laid off to start a business." Yesi continues. "As a result they have to learn everything about starting a business all at once. So the expectation of making money is overwhelming and increases the likelihood of mistakes that they otherwise wouldn't have made under other circumstances." Clearly, the burden of financial necessity can stifle the entrepreneurial spirit in people who aren't entrepreneurs. In other words, the time to start thinking about a new business is while you're employed so the transition isn't as abrupt.

As if she didn't have enough on her plate, Yesi started a company called Proud to Be Latina, whose mission is to break the cycle of poverty and missed opportunities for many women in the Hispanic community. Yesi's goal is to help Hispanic women do this through entrepreneurship and career empowerment. Oh, and I forgot to mention that she's also a director at one of the largest financial powerhouse firms, in addition to being a mother of two boys and a devoted wife. The Pareto Principle aside, Yesi is an example of so many people who strive for something better through entrepreneurship. She started several businesses while keeping her corporate job. Your goal is to start just one. Starting a business will be easier with the right systems in place.

If you're afraid to start a business because you don't believe you have the time, nothing could be further from the truth. You don't have the time because, like many others, you're spending 80 percent of your time on unimportant things. More importantly, there are no systems in place to get you focusing on the 20 percent of activities that will yield 80 percent or more of your revenue for your small business. In other words, you don't have a time problem; you have a productivity problem. We'll explore what you can do specifically to increase productivity so you can focus on starting and growing your business.

Now What?

We've addressed the most common fears and doubts that most people interested in starting a business experience. It's important to remember that starting a business doesn't have to be a complex undertaking. Many of you reading this book want to start a business on the side to supplement your income and perhaps pay off some debt, save for a large purchase, create a sense of financial stability, or start a completely new career. The number of people starting a business after a job loss is steadily increasing, according to the U.S. Census Bureau. (Source: *www.sba. gov/content/small-business-trends*) Sounds inspiring, right? Well, maybe for the entrepreneurs who start successful businesses, but there are a large number of entrepreneurs who fail within their first year. There are millions of new businesses every year and more than half won't make it to their second year! For every successful start-up like "Rent the Runway" or "Stella + Dot," there are exponentially more failures littering the start-up landscape. The American Dream has actually become a nightmare for many entrepreneurs.

Unfortunately many entrepreneurs believe that luck, or a lack thereof, is a major reason for their entrepreneurial failure. The truth is, the major reason small businesses fail is due to lack knowledge in four key areas. These four areas comprise the missing road map that leads entrepreneurs astray and eventually to the failure of their small business.

One of the first things someone will tell you when you want to start a business is that you need a business plan. Indeed, it has become a catch phrase that people repeat in order to sound knowledgeable on the subject of starting a business. In reality, few people know what writing a business plan means or entails. Okay, fewer people know what writing a business plan entails. So they Google "business plan" and scour the Internet for sample plans. Some people even buy business-plan writing software, which can be costly, especially if you're only going to use the software once. If they have the money they'll look for a business-plan writing expert— someone whose expertise is—surprise!—writing a business plan, not starting businesses or even advising entrepreneurs.

Looking for an expert to write your business plan is generally a waste of money because you have to do the majority of the research anyway. The business-plan expert is only taking your input and research and presenting it in a way that follows the "standard" business-plan template. Is the expert knowledgeable about your business? More importantly, what statistics or research do you have that actually validates the assumptions in the business plan?

I spent three weeks writing one of my first business plans in 1999 for a Website/Internet business idea. The world was in an Internet bubble back then. It seemed as though any idea that had the words "Internet" or "dot-com" in it automatically received millions in venture capital money. My idea was a Website that offered athletic apparel, professional sports jerseys, and shoes in Europe. I was targeting the European soccer market and the Internet wasn't as widely used as it was in the States. The first thing I did was spend two weeks creating a business plan.

I didn't write a business plan; I created one, because 97 percent of the information in it was based on assumptions. How did I know how many customers I'd get? How did I know what they would buy and when? What assurances or empirical evidence did I have to increase the likelihood that the business would be a success? I didn't—they were all assumptions based on other companies in that same space. I shopped the business plan and got some interest from an Asian incubator similar to Paul Graham's Y Combinator. A year later, the Internet bubble exploded and the potential term sheet—investment offer—evaporated quicker than water in the Sahara!

The reality is that most business plans suck, and many new entrepreneurs spend too much time writing a business plan (which no one will read) instead of focusing on the four key areas of their business. Remember that Yesi started her businesses without any plans, but she focused on the four key areas—even though she didn't know it at the time. Most successful entrepreneurs focus on the four key areas and, in essence, create a "no-business-plan" business. I'm not saying you shouldn't have a plan; just make sure you know what actually goes into your plan, and remember that creating and writing one may or may not be useful. Yesi built two businesses while working at a full-time job not because she had a business plan, but because she had a vision that encompassed the four key areas

Case Study #1: What people believe a business plan solves

In September of 2012 I received a phone call from a former client who wanted to refer a friend who was looking for business-plan services. His friend Craig needed a business plan to apply for a loan from the bank. The most prudent thing would have been to ask him a few questions. Following are my questions and his responses:

Ebong: What's the business idea?

Craig: Well, it's a new type of chicken and waffles restaurant franchise. There's nothing like that out there and I thought it would be great to start one. (*Craig was being rather secretive with the specific idea, as though he were afraid I'd steal it.*)

Ebong: Do you have experience in the food service industry, and have you managed a restaurant in the past?

Craig: No, I haven't, but I know I can do it!

Ebong: Okay, where do you plan on having your restaurant and what's the area like?

Craig: I wanted it in the Georgetown area (an upscale residential and shopping area in Washington, DC) but the rents will be too high! So I was thinking near Pennsylvania Ave, NE, near the Maryland border.

Ebong: That's a rather significant contrast in terms of location and foot traffic. Tell me about the current location—for example, what's currently in that space? Is there a lot of foot traffic there? Also, whom do you see yourself selling to? Are there chicken places in the area that appear to be busy?

Craig: The current location is a vacant used car lot and there's no real foot traffic, but we can fix it up.

Ebong: Hmm, okay. What are you looking to do with the business plan?

Craig: I want to go to a bank for a loan; my mom will cosign on the loan, as well. She has great credit and believes in my idea.

■■■

Craig called his idea a chicken and waffles food franchise, but more importantly, he thought it was unique. There are plenty of restaurant franchises out there, and they work because the food is good and the owners created processes to ensure replication of the original restaurant experience. In addition, their processes make it easier to train other owners who want to operate their franchises (also known as turn-key operations). I proceeded to dismantle Craig's assumptions and ideas like so:

- Craig has no experience in the food service or restaurant industry, so he would have to learn on the job. This method of learning is expensive because one is learning with one's own money instead of learning from someone who has already had the experience.

- Craig wanted to convert a vacant used-car lot into a restaurant. There was no foot traffic there because the car lot was located far from other shopping centers or stores. Restaurants like McDonald's and Burger King are strong enough brands to entice customers to visit regardless of the location. Their brands were built over decades of services and millions of dollars in commercials and advertising. But no one has heard of Craig's restaurant. The other issue is that it would have been difficult to get the county to agree to the conversion because there would be substantial costs involved in converting a vacant lot into a restaurant where people will eat.

- Craig didn't know what he would charge for the food nor did he know what was unique about his food. In other words, how much could he reasonably charge for meals and make a profit? Since Craig didn't have experience, he didn't know how much money he would need to get started, nor did he know exactly what he would have spent the money on. These are questions the bank manager would have quickly asked...just before telling him to leave the office!

I saved Craig's mother from losing money and possibly learning what bankruptcy is like simply by giving feedback. Writing the business plan would have been an easy way for me to make money, but I would have only accelerated Craig's failure by writing it for him. I'm not asking for a pat on the back. I only want to make it clear that a business plan is rarely the solution. The business plan would have given him a false sense of validation for his idea. You're probably asking yourself, *Aren't business plans important for businesses?* The short answer is yes and no. You can see in the experience I had with Craig that the business plan wouldn't have been a savior but more of a false validation, because the contents of the business plan were wrought with unsubstantiated assumptions and wishes. Unfortunately, many entrepreneurs believe a business plan is all they need to start a viable business. It's not useful if you don't understand what you're writing. Also, no commercial bank manager would have funded a loan for Craig—unless that bank manager wanted to lose his or her job.

In my experience advising small businesses and start-up companies, the main questions bank managers ask are:

- What's the idea, and do you have experience in that area?

- What's your market, and do you know whom you're specifically selling to?

- How much money do you need, and what do you need it for, specifically?

- How will you run the business? For example, will you be an active owner, or is this a franchise?

- What will your sales be in the next two years, and how will you determine that they are at that level?

Actually being an entrepreneur is a lot better than writing about entrepreneurship. As the Founder of Y Combinator, Paul Graham, said "Entrepreneurship is something that is best accomplished by doing." The key is "doing" entrepreneurship as cheaply or as economically as possible without burning through the bank's money! More importantly, as of this writing, banks aren't lending money to new businesses or start-ups. They haven't lent money in years.

No business plan survives first contact with customers.

> —Steve Blank, serial entrepreneur and
> Stanford University professor

There are four major areas—what I call the Four S's—that matter in the majority of successful businesses. Everything else is, as they say in the UK, bollocks. The Four S's are **Structure, Strategy, Systems,** and **Sales,** and they provide the foundation for new and existing businesses. Television programs like ABC's *Shark Tank* demonstrate just how many entrepreneurs fail to grasp all four of these foundational areas. It doesn't matter if you're a freelance graphic designer, an artisan selling crafts on Etsy, an interior designer, or a tech start-up; Structure, Strategy, Systems, and Sales are essential to every small business owner's success. Otherwise, as the song goes, another one bites the dust!

The Four S's are the result of a combination of my experiences working with a wide variety of businesses as a CPA, and working as a corporate/small-business consulting executive. I have spent the last 12 years conceptualizing and then applying these concepts to clients of all sizes. I've also used the experiences of failed businesses to create a simpler conceptual model that can be used to increase the chances of success for every new business. As a result of my growing media platform, I often receive questions about small business from Twitter followers, Facebook friends/fans, and e-mails from entrepreneurs seeking to start, build, and manage their businesses. Some of the more common questions and issues that entrepreneurs face are as follows:

- Bad business idea that solves a problem that doesn't exist or isn't necessary.

- Poorly constructed partnerships or ventures.

- Poor pricing of their product and/or services.

- Sluggish productivity—spending time on tasks that produce neither monetary returns nor value.

- Inadequate sales systems and lack of experience creating sales.

The Four S's are simple and easy to understand because they're not laden with business-speak, management lingo, or the useless analogies found in many other business books. The Four S's provide a necessary road map that millions of American will need when starting their businesses.

There's a large market of entrepreneurs, including women, minorities, and veterans, who are interested in entrepreneurship but who may not have the knowledge or experience in starting a business. Women will create more than half of the 9.72 million new small-business jobs expected to be created by 2018, and more are doing so from home offices across the country. It's a surprising statistic, especially considering that women-owned businesses only comprised 16 percent of all jobs that existed in the United States in 2010. I'm extremely passionate about entrepreneurship and believe the market is ready for new entrepreneurs, given the current economic climate. In addition, I continually receive communiqués of all sorts from small-business owners who are at various stages of their entrepreneurial journey. They only need some guidance to get their business off the ground and realize the American Dream!

There are thousands of average employees, popularly known as cubicle monkeys, sitting in office cubicles doing work they hate for companies they hate. It's difficult to start a business while sitting in an office cube. These budding entrepreneurs work 40 hours or more per week at their paying job and another 40 some-odd hours at night and on weekends on an idea that hasn't paid off yet. As Lori Greiner of ABC's *Shark Tank* said, "Entrepreneurs are willing to work 80 hours a week, to avoid working 40 hours a week." Said another way, entrepreneurs work extremely hard so they don't have to get a job and be beholden to a boss. The amount of time spent working isn't always the problem. The problem is that going from A (the idea) to Z (the product/service/company) appears simple in theory, but it's more difficult in reality, because entrepreneurs don't have the right road map.

Unfortunately, most entrepreneurs make the mistake of neglecting the important steps in between A and Z. That mistake, and the mistake of focusing on assumptions in a business plan that is neither accurate nor useful to the business, leads to failure. Wouldn't it be better to focus on the more important parts of the business than writing a plan that will undoubtedly change? Again, I'm not against business plans per se, but I believe there needs to be a radical change in how we see, write, and use business plans; otherwise we won't be in business for very long, and we'll be encouraging new entrepreneurs to focus on writing a business plan that will contribute to their failure.

Think of all the times you've said the following:

- I hate working at a job I can't stand.
- I hate working for a boss I can't stand.
- I hate working for a company I can't stand.

Because you ostensibly want to start your own business, I'm going to explore the important areas that you'll need to focus on in order to have a chance to be successful. In essence you'll be creating a *more useful* business plan that contributes to your success and sets the parameters in which you will operate. Just because 95 percent of businesses fail doesn't mean that your business has to fail, too. But in order to decrease the likelihood of failure, we first have to identify the small business pitfalls and their causes, which, as you will soon see, isn't easy.

Chapter 2

Invention vs. Innovation

Many people believe that successful businesses must either be a.) the first to market, or b.) better at providing an existing product or service. I have always believed that the latter is generally more important and applicable than the former. For example, Friendster was one of the first social networks. Friendster was founded by computer programmers Jonathan Abrams, Ellen Lee, and Rob Pazornik in 2002, a year before the launch of MySpace (in 2003), and two years before the advent of Facebook (in 2004). Friendster was also one of the first social networking sites to have more than 1 million members sign up. As we all know, it eventually collapsed after catastrophic leadership mistakes and legendary disagreements between the investors and founders. Many of those mistakes fell within the parameters of the Four S's (for example, the poor revenue model, its failure to focus on the needs of customers, and so on). Friendster was eventually surpassed by MySpace and Facebook. MySpace made its own missteps before Facebook quickly vaulted to social networking supremacy and reached a value as high as $100 billion. So you can see that being the first business in a market isn't always the best.

In another example, Google wasn't the first search engine, but it was one of the first to provide targeted "sponsored searches." They created a new market within the search engine industry. For Google's predecessors, search results were mainly keyword driven. As a result, the search results yielded Web pages that contained certain keywords but weren't necessarily relevant to the user. Google knew that a user was more likely to use the search engine again if the results of the search were relevant. It was no longer about finding a bunch of useless Web page links when you used a search engine.

Being the first is important in industries where a zero-sum game exists. A zero-sum game (a term from economic theory) has only one winner; all the other participants are losers. An example of an industry that plays a zero-sum game is the daily deals industry. The company that won (depending on who you talk to, and the jury is still out on this) was either Living Social or Groupon. Both of those companies had to raise hundreds of millions of dollars to exponentially *scale* (grow) very quickly. All the other daily deal sites failed to catch on as there were already two big players in this space. However, chances are your business doesn't fit that market, and therefore being first isn't necessary or as important. There is actually a huge benefit to starting a business after your competitors start theirs. Subsequent competitors in the social media arena learned from the successes and failures of Friendster to provide better products and services. It was also cheaper for subsequent competitors to determine their target market and marketing strategy by paying attention to what didn't work for Friendster. This is an example of why the second principle (*be better at providing an existing product or service*) is generally more accurate and important. Providing an improvement to an existing product or providing exponentially better service can be more lucrative than being first. It also adds more value to the customer. The byproduct of that means you don't have to focus on price competition but the additional value you provide to your customers.

But what if your idea is an invention? Does the same theory apply? Inventions may sound sexy, but innovation generally wins in America today. Innovation is a necessity because the current climate makes it a lot harder to invent new products. From patent protection to creating a prototype, inventing a new product takes a lot of expertise, time, and, most importantly, money. It's easier to create an idea and innovate it than it is to invent a product. Inventing is expensive; most inventions take a long time to come to fruition, and most inventors die poor as a result. The inventors of the Etch-A-Sketch and the printing press serve as cautionary tales regarding the pains and perils of inventions.

A lot goes into inventing a product. This was clearly evident in a small-business forum I take part in on LinkedIn. A woman on the forum, whom I will call Grace, is a licensed physical therapist and healthcare professional. She invented a product for her patients after realizing that there was an easier way to alleviate the pain her patients were experiencing during their recovery from a certain orthopedic procedure. According to Grace's assertions, the product also had ancillary benefits for the patient's recovery. Grace was having difficulty selling the product on a larger scale and getting doctors to prescribe the product to their patients. Inventors often experience this when the new product is outside the range of normal vision for customers. Emphasis must be placed on organic growth of customers or potential users. This generally requires a lot more work and money. In other words, inventing a blockbuster product isn't impossible, but it's difficult. The point here is not to dissuade you from inventing a new product, but to help you think about the best way to start your business by being aware of the potential pitfalls. Doing so will help you hone your idea in such a way as to avoid those pitfalls.

Regardless of whether you're inventing a new product or innovating and improving an idea, small businesses generally fail because they fall prey to one or more of the six major pitfalls. These pitfalls also fall under the umbrella of the Four S's that I mentioned earlier. They are as follows:

1. Complicated business idea (**Structure**)
2. Poor revenue model (**Strategy**)
3. Poor marketing and branding (**Strategy**)
4. Lack of customer acquisition (**Strategy and Sales**)
5. Poor time management (**Systems**)
6. No dedication to a sales formula (**Sales**)

In the next chapter, we'll discuss the first four pitfalls in greater depth.

Chapter 3
Small Business Pitfalls

"There's no other business like this!"

When I was flying home from a recent business trip, the woman in the seat next to me (I'll call her Wanda) asked me what I did for a living. I told to her I was a CPA and small-business consultant. "Wanda" was in the financial services industry. She told me she was happy to know I was a CPA because she was eager to share her new business idea with me and ask for my thoughts. The sense of excitement I felt turned to disappointment when, after her pitch, she said, "There's no other business like this and that's why it will work!" My response to her was, "There's usually a good reason why there's no business like it already!"

"It's generally a myth to think that nothing like this has been tried before," said Geoff Yang, Venture Capitalist at RedPoint Ventures, in a recent entrepreneurial presentation at Stanford (source: Stanford University's Entrepreneurship Corner *http://ecorner.stanford.edu/authorMaterialInfo.html?mid=2993*). Put another way, uniqueness is not a prerequisite for success. Again, there are a lot of unsexy companies currently making millions of dollars every year. There are also a lot of businesses that compete within unsexy industries. There is a plethora of competing maid services and waste-management companies making money and growing. There are countless people sewing aprons and other goods to sell on Etsy.com. These are not sexy businesses, but running a sexy business is not the reason you are getting into entrepreneurship.

You decided to go into business to build something and make money in the process. The better you understand your business idea, the easier it will be to start and grow your business and, more importantly, the better chance you have to succeed in the long term.

Complicated Business Idea

A complicated business idea is generally a poor business idea. Your idea shouldn't have too many assumptions attached to it. A lot of "what-if's" means a lot of room for failure, because these kinds of unknowns require you to rely on a myriad of factors beyond your control. Occam's Razor is famous economic and philosophical theory about decision-making. In short, it says that when faced with a variety of decisions (or in our case, business ideas), choose the one with the least number of assumptions. In other words, when faced with a problem (in this case, how to chose a business idea), the solution with the least number of assumptions is generally the right one. Fewer assumptions in a business idea provides a lower number of variables or "what-if's." As a result, you have more control on the outcome of your business, instead of having to rely on factors beyond your control. Generally, you should be able to explain your business idea in just a few sentences or less. More importantly, your explanation should be in layperson's terms and make sense to the average person—especially if the average person is your customer. Obviously there are exceptions when you are talking about highly technical or scientific ideas—pharmaceuticals or healthcare devices, for example—but that's not what we're talking about here. You have to be able to answer the question: How will I make money with this idea? Being clear on the value or benefit that you provide to customers is the best way to assess whether your idea is worth anything. We'll address this further in a later chapter.

Poor Revenue Model

What is a revenue model? It's actually a very simple yet powerful concept. It will not only dictate whether you'll be able to get your company off the ground, but also whether you will make money from it and last longer than a year. Here is the highly simplified version of a revenue model:

$$(A) - (B) = (C)$$

Wherein A = **Price of Item (Service)**
B = **Cost of Item (Service)**
C = **Gross Profit**
Price of Item – Cost of Item = Gross Profit

If (C) or Gross Profit is a negative number, you're doing something wrong and you'll go out of business, quickly! More specifically, one of two things is wrong: either the price of your product or service is too low, or the cost of making your product is too high.

Every company deals with these problems and it's a constant struggle to either raise your prices, lower your costs, or both. It's a basic equation that should be rooted in facts and numbers. You don't have to like math or be an accountant to understand or use it. For service-based businesses like consulting, getting your pricing and costs right will be even more important. Many entrepreneurs fail to price their services correctly. Entrepreneurs in service-based businesses fail to adequately value their time when starting out and, as we all know, time is money. Poor valuation of time leads to poor pricing which quickly leads to going out of business because you're not making any money. This problem was in evidence by the many small businesses that have used daily deal sites such as Groupon or Living Social. Unfortunately, many of these businesses failed to understand the importance of pricing their products appropriately.

Case Study #2: Pricing and Cost Problems

A small restaurant in the Washington, DC area learned that not pricing one's products correctly and setting up systems can lead to ruin. This business ran a Groupon special but priced its food special too low; moreover, it didn't account for the cost of using Groupon. Groupon was great for the restaurant because its customer base greatly increased, but it literally lost money with every customer it served. The numbers showed that it would have been better for the restaurant to go out of business and not run the Groupon special because it lost more money running the special. It was literally paying people to eat at the restaurant instead of the other way around! The point is simple: Groupon is a great sales and marketing tool if used correctly, but you have to know your costs, pricing, and gross profit in order for it to benefit your business. You also have to make sure you have the proper systems in place before running a daily deal special. The power of a Groupon or a Living Social is its ability to leverage its large network of customers and direct them to your business based on interests. Accounting for the potential overwhelming customer reaction is important and should have been addressed before running the special.

Poor Marketing and Branding

"Build a better mousetrap and the world will beat a path to your door!" Many new entrepreneurs believe people will automatically come to their business when they launch their company's Website or open their doors. Companies and Websites are plentiful, so launching one never automatically equates to hoards of customers lining up at your door. People will not come to your company or buy your products and services unless you give them a good reason to do so. The goal is to get customers engaged in your business by solving their problems—but how do you do that? Companies with large marketing budgets spend huge amounts of money to get customers to buy their products. Can you afford to spend $4 million dollars for a 30-second commercial spot during the Super Bowl? In the past you would be in a world of trouble if your competitor could afford to spend that amount of money and you couldn't. That meant your competitor could also afford to market and advertise in lesser expensive areas and on a wider scale, such as on billboards and in magazines.

Fortunately, times have changed, and it's easier than ever to share your message with the world using social media. Visionaries like Gary Vaynerchuk have shown how powerful social media can be, if—and that's a big if—it's used correctly. Social media is great for marketing and branding, but as it is in any other medium, customer engagement is essential and more important than visual spamming. Visual spammers are companies that post unfocused and advertorial content on social media avenues. After a while, followers tune them out, unfollow, and unfriend.

To engage your customers and keep them interested, you have to provide either a better or a different solution. Customers are looking for useful content that enriches their lives. Your solution should pinpoint and then solve a painful problem the customer has. The growth of every product or service is generally based on these basic principles, and millions of small businesses have failed because they failed to understand these principles.

You can look at Twitter and Facebook today and find companies posting useless advertisements to followers and fans. These companies erroneously call this advertising and marketing but it is actually bullshit. It is rather annoying and after a while, customers simply stop listening and watching. Sharing useful information with your followers and friends will increase the likelihood of engagement and retainment.

Lack of Customer Acquisition

Evolution is important to your business. Companies need to seek new opportunities to grow their customer base without relying on existing and repeat customers. Relying on your core product or client is fine in the beginning, but that strategy is detrimental to long-term success. Kodak is a great example. As the market moved toward digital cameras, Kodak failed to grow outside of the photographic film industry, and the company that was once worth as much as $50 billion had to sell many of its patents and exit several of its businesses to emerge from bankruptcy in 2013. Kodak's mistake was relying on the industry of photographic film rather than expanding into developing areas.

It's important to see patterns where people see chaos, so that you can identify the next logical step. You will then feel compelled to stand in front of that market.

—Geoff Yang

Chapter 4
The Four S's: Structure

Structure is the first category we'll cover in the Four S's. I've personally seen many small businesses suffer and fail because this area was overlooked when the business was started. Businesses of all kinds struggle with this concept and end up derailing their entrepreneurial train as soon as it's left the start-up station. The Bible states that man cannot live by bread alone; the same applies in your business. A business cannot survive on the idea alone, but on the foundation, or structure, upon which your business was built. The structure of your business encompasses your idea *and* forms the foundation of your business's success.

Evaluating Your Idea

To use an ice hockey analogy from Wayne Gretzky, too many people are skating to where the puck was, not where it will be. Once a trend has been identified, people rush to copy the "hot" new idea. The marketplace then gets littered with similar businesses trying to do the same thing as the market leaders, but those similar businesses have little market share. Competitors rush to make the Hispanic version of Groupon or the daily deal site that focuses only on college students. Why bother? The market leaders can easily create the exact same segment they are in and crush them. There is no barrier to entry, which is not necessarily a large issue, but it becomes one when your success is predicated on having large volumes of customers. Market leaders have the infrastructure, the funding, the systems, and the media buzz to do it. They do not have to buy your company and they will not compete with you. They will simply crush you. For example, after the successes of Groupon and Living Social, the Web quickly became littered with group discount sites that promised cheaper deals for subscribers. The businesses who copied Groupon and Living Social did not have the hundreds of millions of dollars needed to rapidly grow and compete with the leaders. Groupon and Living Social raised large sums of money and acquired competitors in other markets where those competitors were the market leaders. The first movers, or the first businesses that grew the fastest in this space, won. Entrepreneurs who "get" this tend to see the next logical step in a world of chaos. They don't spend time trying to replicate a market that is already oversaturated.

Here's a simplistic illustration that highlights the necessity of seeing the opportunities ahead and the next logical steps. Joe sees a pair of wings and believes they'll make the best wings ever. Tracy sees feathers and also believes they are the best feathers ever. Tony sees a beak. Sam, however, notices that the combination of everyone's description is actually a bird. Sam also notices that birds can be used as a method of communication in the form of carrier pigeons. Sam starts a business using this idea of the next logical step. Many entrepreneurs lose sight of the bigger picture, while the successful ones are more like Sam. Geoff Yang, a venture capitalist with RedPoint Ventures, calls this *pattern recognition*. The recognition of patterns in the marketplace can be lucrative if executed correctly.

Finding the Pain Point

So what if you *can* see the bigger picture? How do you apply that concept to evaluating your own idea for a business? More importantly, what customer problem will your business idea solve? (Hint: The severity of the customer problem increases your chances of success.) This reminds me of a recent speech I heard from friend and visionary Reggie Aggarwal. Reggie is the son of Indian immigrants and a lawyer turned successful entrepreneur. He's also the founder and CEO of Cvent, Inc. Cvent is a Software as a Service (SaaS) provider of event management and e-mail marketing software solutions to thousands of companies. Cvent is the largest event meeting venue and e-mail marketing firm in the United States. If you've been invited to a corporate event, chances are your invitation was created and sent using Cvent's software. You've probably used his company's software or services if you've ever had to plan a corporate event for a company.

Reggie's speech was inspiring because it encompassed the highs and lows of his journey from near bankruptcy (corporate and personal) to triumph and success. The biggest lesson for me came at the beginning of his speech and was in alignment with the Structure portion of the Four S's. The biggest lesson from Reggie's speech was this: Your chances of entrepreneurial success greatly increase when your company or idea solves an identifiable problem, or customer pain point. What customer pain point are you solving? Not all ideas will make good businesses. Not all problems are worth solving. More importantly, not all businesses solve problems or address pain points. We'll discuss the concept of the pain point in greater depth in the following chapter.

Chapter 5

The Pain Point: Aspirin vs. Vitamin

Let's say you live on the fourth floor of a four-story apartment building that doesn't have an elevator, only stairs. You have to walk up and down several flights of stairs every time you leave or return to the apartment. Every normal work day, you have to walk several blocks to get to the Subway station. After walking out of your apartment building one morning, you realize that you have a splitting headache. Would you run back upstairs to grab some aspirin? Now let's say you realize you forgot to take your multivitamin after walking out. How many of you would run back upstairs for that? Chances are most of you would run back upstairs to grab aspirin for your splitting headache, but wouldn't do that just for a vitamin. The aspirin solves a pressing need—your headache. The multivitamin isn't a pressing need, but a convenience for health. The pain point for you is your headache, and the aspirin is the solution for that pain point.

When you apply this to running a business, solving a pain point (addressing a pressing need) increases your chances of success because you're solving an identifiable problem. Solving that pain point also makes it easier to explain to your customers why they should buy your product or use your services at a premium price. Very few customers will argue or negotiate a lower price if the value you're providing exceeds their need to save a few dollars. Solving an identifiable and pressing problem makes it easier to educate your customers on the benefits of your product or service, differentiate your company from your competitors, and increase the likelihood of a successful business. Can you hone your idea so that it's an aspirin instead of a vitamin?

Here's another example. Your toilet water line breaks in the middle of the night and starts to flood your house. You call an emergency plumber who charges $300 for after-hour house calls. The $300 is negligible if it means you can avoid having substantial water damage in your house. As a customer, you see greater value in resolving the water leak issue than you do trying to nickel and dime the plumber. The alternative hurts a lot more! Remember Reggie Aggarwal from the previous chapter? To be clear, the aspirin vs. vitamin example wasn't necessarily created by Reggie; it was, however, the first time I'd heard it put that way.

Entrepreneurs who create a product or service based on a recurring or pressing need have a better chance of succeeding. Sure, the Pet Rock, Cabbage Patch Kids, and Beanie Babies—all wildly successful businesses—didn't create recurring sales, nor were they sustainable businesses in the long run. They certainly weren't solving a problem or alleviating a pain point. They were merely novelties, and novelties aren't recurring or sustainable. What real problem are you solving? You have to be able answer that question; otherwise, your company will go the way of the Pet Rock!

Reggie's pain point was he needed to send multiple personal e-mails to executives in addition to booking meeting venues for his entrepreneurial groups. Through his experiences, he realized that companies had the same issues he did in collecting and manipulating the e-mail addresses of customers, in addition to acquiring meeting venues. He was able to remove several steps from the process and save companies money in the process. That's how Cvent was born, and it's why Cvent is still thriving today. He identified a real problem and, in doing so, revealed his target market. Reggie then solved that problem and alleviated his customers' pain point. The business idea came from the opportunity and timing of the pain point. The goal is to create a sustainable idea from seeing a potential opportunity and make sure the need for that opportunity matches the timing of the opportunity.

Kauffman Foundation Senior Fellow Ted Zoller once said that "entrepreneurship is the intersection of opportunity and need" (source: *http:// ecorner.stanford.edu/authorMaterialInfo.html?mid=2882*).

I would submit that *three* major factors are essential for your idea to have real potential:

1. Opportunity.

2. Customer benefits (what problem or pain point are you solving?).

3. Timing.

Your idea doesn't have to be sexy! Your idea doesn't have to be unique or insanely different. You also don't have to be a genius to start a business (unless you're starting Google or developing a cure for cancer). The important thing is to determine whether your business idea is any good and then analyze the likelihood of success for your idea.

Idea Validation

Entrepreneurs often lack enough confidence in their ideas to attempt executing them. To counteract this lack of confidence, there's an important concept I call *idea validation*. This encompasses everything you need to consider when starting your business. One of the easiest ways to validate your idea is to determine the small segment of the population that will most likely buy your product or service. Targeting the specific group that will actually pay you money for your idea, product, or service is the first step. These days, it's cheaper to test your idea by using a variety of methods, including crowd sourcing. So throwing spaghetti against the wall to see what sticks is no longer a plausible strategy for starting a business! The goal is to get your first *paying* customer who needs your services.

In the next chapter, we'll talk about how to figure out where your idea will fall in the quality hierarchy, and what that means for you, practically speaking.

Chapter 6
Idea Hierarchy Model

Ideas for businesses are plentiful. Almost everyone has had a small-business idea at some point in their lives. The secret sauce of a winning business is in the execution; however, the *quality* of the idea increases the likelihood of successfully executing that idea and seeing it to fruition. I believe there are different levels of ideas, an "idea hierarchy" that you should consider when evaluating your idea and whether it has "legs."

The idea hierarchy is a simple representation of the four levels of the quality of your idea. The hierarchy goes from the best to worst, top to bottom:

1. Niche ideas.
2. Established brands.
3. Novelty items or non-recurring ideas.
4. Useless ideas and premature ideas (whose time has not yet come).

Niche Ideas

Solving a problem for a particular niche and being very selective about the market you are targeting will increase the chances that your business will succeed. I once had a conversation with an economics major from George Mason University about business ideas and markets. During our conversation, I mentioned my belief in the importance of having a niche:

Me: I believe it's important to have a very narrow focus on your market when you start a business.

Student: I disagree, because wouldn't that limit your business and whom you sell to?

Me:	Yes, that's my point exactly.
Student:	That makes no sense, though. The goal is to grow your business, not limit it!
Me:	Agreed! But if you start a business with your own money, you can't service a large population anyway. Scaling isn't your current problem or concern. Your concern is to get your first paying customer.
Student:	That's true.
Me:	In addition, spreading yourself too thin leads to an erosion of the quality of your services and goods. It would be easier to grow by becoming the best in a particular area, after which you can then grow into other markets. Most companies that grow, start that way.

Established Brands

Established brands have the luxury of creating a niche and/or moving to the masses. These brands have spent years and perhaps millions of dollars establishing and building their name. A brand is more than a logo, a symbol, or a catch phrase. A strong brand encompasses experiences and emotions (for example, feelings of nostalgia). As esteemed matchmaking expert and media entrepreneur Paul Carrick Brunson said to me, "Your brand is what you say when you can't say anything." Certain words probably enter your mind when you see a Mercedes Benz drive by—luxury, style, and "very expensive." The same words are evoked when you see a woman wearing a pair of Christian Louboutin shoes (you can tell they are Louboutins by the iconic red soles). It takes a lot of money and, in some cases, market luck to build a trend which eventually becomes an established brand. This applies not only to your business's services and products, but also to the representatives of that business. One without the other is useless!

Novelty Items or Non-Recurring Ideas

If you watch TV with any regularity, you've probably seen the infomercial for the Snuggie. As much as people use the Pet Rock or the Snuggie as examples of successful ideas, they are not. These products and similar ideas aren't real businesses because a business requires the ability to be self-sufficient and sustaining. If your goal is to create a product that you can hopefully sell one million units of, then you're most likely going to fail. Actually, you're definitely going to fail.

I recently spoke at a women's conference about small business, the Four S's, and innovative ways to fund your business. After the break-out session, I spoke with an entrepreneur who had an interesting product idea. There was a market for it, and it was something that I could see many Americans using while they travel. She wanted to talk to me about marketing ideas and scaling of the business. Ten minutes later I asked her where she saw her business going, and she said, "Well, if the Snuggie can sell four million units, I can do the same!" The Snuggie shouldn't be a benchmark or barometer for your business idea. I told her that she only has a product, not a business. More importantly, until she comes up with an idea that solves a tangible problem, she should consider selling or licensing her product.

Useless Ideas and Premature Ideas

Useless ideas (ideas don't solve an apparent problem) are at the bottom of the heap. In addition, the ideas whose time has not yet come (because of poor infrastructure or technology, for example) are also at the bottom of the hierarchy. This level is literally the opposite or inverse of the niche level because these kinds of ideas don't solve problems nor do they have a market worth pursuing.

In 2005, my business partner and I started a company that sought to allow people to use their cell phones to make payments and receive deals via location-based data on their phone. In other words, our company was trying to create an app before apps even existed. The technology in the mobile space wasn't available yet. Many people were still using archaic phones and the iPhone wasn't out yet. We pitched our idea to venture capital and angel investors. All of them understood and liked the concept, but when you're too early to the start-up party, you lose. As they say, timing is (almost) everything!

In the next chapter, we'll talk about the very best ideas, those that focus on a small niche market and increase your chances of success.

Chapter 7

What's Your Niche?

One of the best ways to increase your chances of success is to define your niche market. A niche market is a specific section of a larger market. Finding a niche market requires you to focus your efforts to a specific group defined by a variety of characteristics. These characteristics, generally called *demographics*, describe the people within that particular, specific group of a larger market. In other words, you have to focus on a very specific cross-section of people when you start out. Here are some of the many benefits in defining your niche market:

- **Market research:** You perform market research at the same time that you identify your niche market. For example, if you're a Web designer who focuses primarily on Websites built in particular content management platform (CMS), such as Wordpress, you can easily determine the issues those particular clients are having. More importantly, you can spend less time trying to be all things to all people and focus on the forums, Meet-ups, or groups that love using Wordpress. You also have the ability to learn more about the demographic of your niche like the ages, the industries your clients are focused on, and the level of sophistication your clients have.

- **Fewer capital requirements:** You will need less capital to market and promote your idea when you focus on a specific niche. Using the Web designer example, you can choose specific search engine optimization words that fit your niche. If your focus is on lawyers and law firms, you can chose keywords such as "lawyer" instead of a more general terms such as "business." Using fewer keywords will mean less money spent on search engine optimization to get started.

- **Increased pricing:** Targeting your niche allows you to focus on the particular needs of that market, which means you can often charge a premium for your goods or services.

- **Provide great service or product:** Less time and fewer resources spent servicing other areas means you can focus primarily on your niche market and provide it with excellent service.

Choosing a Niche Is Imperative!

Choosing a niche for your business is imperative to your success. You significantly lower the chances of success by not choosing one. There is a popular saying, "Jack of all trades, master of none." This is often used to describe a person who has many skills but isn't an expert in any one area. This describes many, if not most entrepreneurs, and unfortunately it can accelerate failure. A jack of all trades is average and indiscernible from every other person in his market. You can't provide the best service to your customers if you have to focus on a wider range of services. It is no different than opening the Yellow Pages and choosing a service provider.

Have you ever been to a restaurant or diner where the menu had 10 or more pages, and each page was filled from top to bottom with a dizzying array of items? Unless Gordon Ramsey was in the kitchen, there's absolutely no way the chef could prepare all of the food on that menu. That means everything suffers and the food is just average. A jack of all trades is an average, skilled person. Average skilled people and companies aren't paid well. Average skilled people and companies aren't respected. Why should they be paid well or respected? There are a heck of a lot of others just like them littering the marketplace. The question is, how can you get paid well, receive respect, and not litter the marketplace?

The best solution is to become an expert in a subsection of your field. Many professionals specialize in a target subsection of their craft or profession. As an example, lawyers often specialize in a particular segment of law, including civil, criminal, maritime, real estate, and immigration law. Malcolm Gladwell, author of the *New York Times* bestseller *Outliers,* devoted a chapter to mergers and acquisitions pioneer Joseph Flom. What was interesting was how Flom came to specialize in corporate mergers and acquisitions. Flom interviewed with several large law firms after graduating from Harvard Law school in 1948 but was denied employment due to his Jewish pedigree. These firms were akin to private golf clubs that routinely denied employment to graduates who lacked the "correct" religious affiliation and family background. More importantly, these firms also represented the country's largest and most established companies.

At the time, many of the large law firms did not do corporate litigation and corporate takeovers. These firms would bring in Flom whenever a corporate raider made a run at one of their establishment clients. In the 1970s it was easier to borrow money because federal regulations were more relaxed. This created a boom in corporate takeovers. Soon every firm wanted to handle hostile takeovers, but Flom was the expert in the space. He saw an opportunity to specialize in an important aspect of corporate litigation before corporate raiding, mergers, and acquisitions became a normal method of operation. It is virtually impossible to be a competent lawyer in all of those areas, and without specialization, becoming highly sought after and successful is difficult.

How many of you know experts in your field? How did they become experts and why are they well-known? These experts have skillfully differentiated themselves from the rest of the market. In other words, they are above average and highly sought after. Focusing on a niche and specializing in a particular area increase the chances that you will succeed and grow.

Every large company that you know today most likely started as a niche business. They were able to grow into a larger company after dominating their niche, providing the best service and becoming a market leader. Here are a few examples:

- Facebook: originally started as a social network for Harvard students only.
- Google: originally started as a more intuitive search engine that focused on increasing the likelihood of receiving relevant search results.

- Apple: originally started as a personal computer company but has since grown into providing customers with portable digital listening devices (iPods), phones, computers, online storage (iCloud), and digital music delivery (iTunes), just to name a few.

In sum, defining and focusing on a niche allows you to:

- Dominate your market.

- Provide the best services to your customers as a result of focusing on a few.

- Become an expert in your particular market which increases the likelihood of free publicity and media appearances.

- Acquire your first customer and make money to fund future operations.

In the next chapter, we'll discuss what you need to do to become an expert in your niche.

Chapter 8

Become an Expert in Your Niche

Becoming an expert in your specific niche requires time and is important to the success of your business. Flom's ability to grow his firm (Skadden, Arps) and dominate corporate takeovers, mergers, and acquisitions was predicated on becoming an expert in his field. In my case, being offered a professional basketball contract was dependent on my full understanding of the process and decorum of European professional basketball. I spent months constantly learning, reading, and speaking to other professionals in that area in order to acquire the skills I needed to receive a pro contract.

Many people fail because they simply don't do the necessary work. It is not easy to have a successful business and become an expert. Do you have to become an expert in order to start a business? No, you don't, but becoming an expert or subject-matter expert makes it easier to alleviate customers' concerns about your expertise. Robert Cialdini's best-selling book *Influence: The Psychology of Persuasion* identifies this psychological trigger as *authority*. (I discuss his book in further depth in Chapter 19.)

Here is how you can become an expert:

▶ Search for popular books, blogs, and information by leaders in your field.

▶ Continue to interact with experts in your field and ask questions about their business. For example, ask them how they started, what pitfalls they encountered, and what steps they took to overcome those pitfalls.

▶ Practice the trade in your niche! Sounds simple enough, but you should produce actual content that relates to your industry. For example, I learned a lot about pro basketball and I engaged with others on a popular professional basketball Website forum called EuroBasket.com.

▶ Dedicate several hours a week to read about your industry and acquire additional skills and information. Every successful entrepreneur I have met has told me they set time aside for reading and continuing education about their industry. Doing this can provide you with a better perspective on serving your customers.

Media Expert: Sonya Gavankar

I want to highlight the importance of focusing on a niche, becoming an expert, and getting your message to that niche audience. A friend of mine named Sonya e-mailed me recently for some input on adding more structure to her media training business. She had recently been inundated with requests for help in media training. Sonya is a former beauty pageant winner who competed in the Miss America Pageant as Ms. District of Columbia. She also consults with and trains current pageant contestants. Sonya is an award-winning television personality who can be seen hosting programs on PBS, BGTV, and MHz networks. Her career has spanned diverse programs, covering everything from international food shows to hard news. Sonya serves as the face of the Newseum by hosting live interview programs, appearing in video installations, and video blogs and game shows. She brings a cohesive voice to the Newseum's 250,000 square feet of exhibits and interactive programming. In other words, she is an expert!

Sonya wanted to create a services rate card to share with her new clients. Historically she would just tell her clients her prices, and her clients would decide what they wanted. These were her first thoughts (actual pricing has been changed to protect confidentiality):

Old Copy

With the need to fill a 24-hour news cycle and create online content, more media outlets are turning to business professionals for expertise. Be prepared for when this call comes by preparing ahead of time for live studio and taped interviews.

Sonya Gavankar is an award-winning television personality and can help you prepare for television by fine tuning your presentation for the unique medium. Even if you are an expert presenter, TV has unique challenges that she can prepare you for.

Sonya will work with you via e-mail to assess up to three of your existing videos: $100.

Sonya will work with you in person over a 45 minute consultation to discuss your unique style, using two of your existing videos: $500.

Sonya will teach you how to quickly and easily read a teleprompter for presentations to large groups: $500.

Add on an additional 30 minute mock interview practice and real time video assessment to any of the above: $200.

Sonya and her team will help you create a production plan for video presentation: $800 to $1,000.

Following is my feedback and what we ended up with:

New Copy

Are you a business professional about to appear on TV?

Do you have to give presentations in front of large groups?

Television and media interviews can greatly boost your organization's public image if taught from the right source!

More television networks are turning to experts like you to provide analysis and expertise for news stories. Even if you are an expert presenter, TV has unique challenges that you need to be prepared for.

With the need to fill a 24-hour news cycle and create online content, more media outlets are turning to business professionals for expertise. Be prepared for when this call comes by preparing ahead of time for live studio and taped interviews.

Sonya Gavankar is an award-winning television personality and can help you prepare for television by fine tuning your presentation for this unique medium.

— Packages —

Analysis and Feedback of Prior Appearances: $250
Useful feedback is imperative for successful media training. Sonya will analyze and provide feedback via e-mail for up to 3 of your previous appearance / videos.

Live Consultation and Media Assessment: $750
Sonya will provide up to 45 minutes of live and in person consultation to discuss your unique style using 2 of your existing videos.

Teleprompter Consultation and Techniques: $750
Using a teleprompter can be a large challenge but Sonya will use her experience and unique techniques to teach you how to quickly and easily read a teleprompter for presentations to large groups.

Add Additional Time to Teleprompter Package - $300
Add on an additional 30 minute mock interview practice and real time video assessment to any of the above.

Video Presentation Production Plan - $1,500
Sonya and her team will help you create a production plan for video presentation. The price of this package is normally $4,500 but you can have your video presentation ***professionally*** created, edited, and produced for a third of the price!

The Upshot

I wanted to highlight three main areas in the copy for this flyer:

1. What fears and problems do your services solve? The majority of people fear public speaking and giving presentations. That fear exponentially increases when you introduce television appearances. Television networks are constantly looking for business professionals to serve as experts for their television shows.

2. Who specifically needs your services? Business professionals who want to present themselves as experts and bring exposure to their business.

3. Do you currently have the necessary experience in the areas/industry that has the problem? Sonya is considered an expert who has the necessary training and expertise to teach media training. Becoming an expert or authority is an important concept and psychological trigger, as discussed in Robert Cialdini's famed best-selling book *Influence: The Psychology of Persuasion*.

The main focus of the one-pager was to highlight how Sonya's experience solves the biggest fears of business professionals. The fear of media and corporate presentations far exceeds the need of these business professionals to hoard their money. This is why it was beyond imperative to focus on providing extreme value to these clients. When a potential client or customer says, "That's a lot of money for those services," you should reply by saying, "I produce results. After working together, you will not only be able to give presentations and appear on television, but you will increase the exposure of and marketing for your company."

The other issue that came up was raising your prices after your first few clients. We are treated as we are perceived. If a customer perceives you as a *fungible* (an expendable or replaceable commodity), you will be treated as such. The customer will neither value you nor your services. Raising your prices also weeds out the bad customers—the ones who don't see the value in your services and those who don't pay on a timely basis.

Marketing Expert: Yanik Silver

Here's another example to illustrate the important relationship between becoming an expert and raising your prices. Several months ago, I had breakfast with my friend and mentor Yanik Silver. Yanik is a highly successful entrepreneur, a best-selling author, and a digital marketing expert. In addition, Yanik is the founder of Maverick Business Adventures, an invitation-only club for high net worth and adventurous entrepreneurs.

I first met Yanik as a guest of Derek and Melanie Coburn, who are the founders of networking mastermind group, Cadre DC. Cadre DC offers successful professionals a new approach to networking by sharing expertise, exchanging ideas, and connecting professionals from other networks. Cadre DC is a great experience because the chances of meeting successful entrepreneurs and individuals are about as high as you can get, about 100 percent.

I was familiar with Yanik's success and story before meeting him, but I wanted to hear his story directly from him. Like Gary Vaynerchuk (another great entrepreneurial mentor I will discuss later), Yanik emigrated from Russia as a young child. Through most of his young life, Yanik started selling for his father's medical devices supply company. A light bulb went off when he realized the methods doctors used to market their services were archaic. In 1998, Silver used his experiences to craft targeted marketing ads to sell goods. With no Internet, Yanik faxed (yes, faxed) a sales letter to one of his cosmetic surgeon clients promising that his $900-plus marketing course would increase revenues. Yanik received his first order before he even created the course! By the time he was 26, he was making $10,000 to $15,000 a month teaching physicians how to improve their sales. Yanik realized that as the Internet bubble was bursting, there was a growing market in targeted e-commerce sites. He subsequently created an instant sales letters course that taught readers how to sell products online. His marketing courses and information products business made Yanik a millionaire by age 30!

There are three lessons you can learn from Yanik:

1. **The importance of becoming an expert in your niche.** It is important to become an expert in your niche or at least have the experience to do the work. Knowing your niche well provides you with the ability to anticipate the next step in your business. As Geoff Yang said, it makes it easier for pattern recognition. You save time and money because you don't have to learn the basics and can focus on what areas are lacking. You can also anticipate the future of your business without remaining stuck in the minutiae of daily operations.

2. **The importance of testimonials and feedback.** Sonya and Yanik received feedback and validation for their business ideas. In Yanik's case, he sent out test marketing to solicit orders and feedback from potential customers. Many entrepreneurs waste their time and money creating products and services before they know if people even want them.

3. **The importance of raising your prices because of the value you bring.** Yanik agreed that providing more value to customers allows you to raise your prices. The $900 was negligible compared to tens of thousands of dollars in new clients he brought in.

How to Find Your Niche

Finding your niche market requires identifying the pain point of that particular market. Identifying the pain point increases your chances of lasting success while your niche market helps you narrowly focus on pricing and services. I worked with a Web developer client named Harmony who wanted some help with marketing and growing her business. Her business was simple: build Websites for professionals and provide them with ancillary web/IT services. Harmony realized that her clients and new referrals were primarily from the professional minority community. More specifically, her market was comprised of budget conscious African-American female professionals interested in IT and Web services

Okay, we've identified our niche market, but how do you determine the pain point? That's not as easy! Believe it or not, it involves using your elevator pitch.

To build a brand, narrow the focus!
　　　　　　　—Al Ries, of marketing firm Ries and Ries

In the next chapter, we'll figure out whether your idea makes sense and is viable, simply by using your elevator pitch.

Chapter 9
The Elevator Pitch

As you probably know, an elevator pitch is a short summary used to quickly and simply define a product, service, or organization and its benefits to customers. The term "elevator pitch" reflects the idea that it should be possible to deliver the summary in the time span of an elevator ride, or approximately 30 seconds to two minutes.

Your elevator pitch should be simple and concise. Make sure you avoid platitudes, excessive adjectives, and other filler. I've heard a lot of these kinds of elevator pitches from some of my small-business and start-up clients. Drop words and phrases like "innovative" and "one of a kind." To me, the worst and most nauseating word is "revolutionary." The railroad, refrigerators, and the Internet were revolutionary; your idea probably isn't. Here's an example of what I mean: "AquaFree is a revolutionary and innovative product that sanitizes clothes without water!" Don't use this kind of hyperbole because as intriguing as your idea sounds, remember that you're not impartial.

Here is an example of an elevator pitch that I recently received from a client named Rachel:

Elevator Pitch From Small Business Client: XYZ, LLC

> *Simple, straightforward, goal-focused Web design for trade professionals and service businesses, with a focus on helping woman- and minority-owned companies. We also help businesses get started with foundational, long-lasting marketing strategies.*

This example is horrible, and you'll see why shortly. The goal of an elevator pitch is to give your audience a simple and concise summary of your business. It shouldn't be difficult to understand or share. Your elevator pitch should also encompass simple principles that answer the following questions:

- What is the name of your company or product?
- What does your company or product do?
- What problem does your service/product solve?
- What is the major benefit your customer experiences by using your product or service?

By answering these questions, we can create a clearer and more concise elevator pitch.

Elevator Pitch That Answers the Previous Questions

> *XYZ, LLC is a Web design firm providing Web and marketing services to women and minority professionals and their service based businesses. Our turnkey services make it easier for these professionals to focus on their businesses and not IT issues.*

The elevator pitch is only the first step. Now we need specifics. We'll use these three major factors—Opportunity, Customer Benefits, and Timing—to expand your idea and determine if it's workable:

1. **Opportunity: What problem(s) are you solving? Explain the current need or opportunity that your business will solve or capitalize on.**

   There is a void in the marketplace between very cheap Website solutions and very expensive solutions. The cheap solutions provide "drag and drop" options with little to no customizations. The other option includes hiring a high-priced design firm which isn't feasible for most new or small companies. We make it easier for a minority professional (lawyer, CPA, doctor, plumber) or those in service businesses to build a customizable Website for a great price.

2. **Customer Benefits: What is your solution to this problem? How will your business solve the problem?**

   We created packages with the following solutions:

- Website templates that feature more customizations. For example, the client can customize the location of logos, Website content, and colors.
- Search Engine Optimization (SEO) consulting for one hour.
- Integration of e-mail/newsletter marketing and e-mail list manager (such as Constant Contact).
- Competing on price and customer service.

3. Timing: Why does the marketplace need your business now?

Rachel from XYZ realized that there were a lot more women and minorities who were struggling with Website creation in Rachel's community. In addition, Rachel has a background in Web design and marketing, so entrepreneurs in the community continually ask her questions about Websites.

Here's another example that illustrates the importance of Opportunity and Timing. Opportunity and Timing played a tremendous role in another entrepreneurial venture I embarked on in 2008. As a CPA working for a number of large companies, I was required to dress professionally. Finding stylish clothes that fit wasn't easy because I'm 6 feet 5 inches tall. As a former professional and college basketball player, I had a lot of friends who faced similar challenges. So I started a made-to-measure clothing line in 2008. I had the manufacturing and fabric sourcing but the idea was to feature a business model similar to Build-a-Bear.

After a brief online tutorial, customers could go online to enter their measurements, choose a style of suit, shirts, and trousers and pay for them. Since the operation was "Just In Time" or "On Demand," there was no inventory or other large fixed costs. Despite the tremendous amount of public support and media publicity, the company struggled for a variety of reasons, and I made the easy decision to close the business after two years.

Fast forward to 2013. I met a fashion entrepreneur at a social event who was a contestant of a fashion oriented reality show on a major network. He asked me about my experience in the fashion industry and why I closed the business. I was frank about the challenges I faced dealing with the fashion industry and how difficult it was to grow a brand. The entrepreneur continued to share with me that he had generated traction with his clothing line and several celebrities were now wearing his label.

Here are three important reasons Opportunity and Timing were important for my niche and idea:

1. Customers were not yet comfortable with ordering expensive made-to-measure clothing online. More importantly, customers were not comfortable with their ability to accurately measure themselves.

2. Less intricate clothing such as trousers and shirts work better online than suits. (Online clothing retailers such as Bonobos and Hugh & Crye are examples of this truism.)

3. Reality shows serve as platforms for contestants and cast members. As of this writing there are several reality shows on a variety of networks that focus on the fashion industry.

Interactive: Your Turn! What's Your Idea?

Write your elevator pitch and idea in three sentences or fewer:

How can you be successful if you cannot explain the purpose of your business to the average person? If customers cannot understand what you offer, they will not buy from you. It's difficult to raise money or obtain loans if you can't explain your idea in simple terms either. This part of the Structure area is important because it helps you focus on the three components necessary to evaluate your idea.

Now that you have a better understanding of your idea, what's next? Now we have to talk about entity structure!

Chapter 10
Entity Structure

One of the first tasks an entrepreneur has to deal with is deciding what kind of business entity to form. There are several types of entities that you can choose for your new business. For example, these entities are corporations, partnerships, and sole proprietorships. We'll start with the limited liability company.

Limited Liability Company

A single-member Limited Liability Company, or LLC, may be a good choice if you're starting a new business and you're the sole owner. A flexible business entity, an LLC is a hybrid containing elements of both partnerships and corporations. The primary characteristic an LLC shares with a corporation is limited liability, and the primary characteristic it shares with a partnership is the availability of pass-through income taxation. LLCs are popular because, similar to a corporation, owners have limited personal liability for the debts and actions of the LLC. It's important to keep in mind that owners of LLCs do not always have liability protection. Many courts have pierced the corporate veil when the owners of the LLC are engaged in fraud or misrepresentation. The corporate veil may also be pierced if there is little to no separation between the LLC and its owners/members. Therefore, it is advantageous to maintain a separate set of accounting books and bank accounts, because mingling of funds can give the impression of "owner operating as alter-ego."

The owners of an LLC are called members. Since most states do not restrict ownership, members may include individuals, corporations, other LLCs, and foreign entities. Unlike a subchapter S-corporation, there is no maximum number of members or owners. A single-member LLC is an LLC that only has one owner. Single-member LLCs do not have to file a separate income tax return for federal tax purposes. The income and expenses of the LLC flow directly to the single member's individual tax return. A few types of businesses generally cannot be LLCs, such as banks and insurance companies. Check your state's requirements and the federal tax regulations for further information. There are special rules for foreign LLCs, which most likely aren't applicable to you.

Advantages of LLCs

Following are some advantages of LLCs:

- **Pass-through taxation**—The LLC doesn't pay tax and the tax is passed through to the owner(s) so there is only one level of tax.

- **Limited liability**—The owners of the LLC are not personally liable for the debts of the LLC.

- **LLCs are enduring legal business entities**—The life of the LLC can extend beyond the illness or even death of its owner(s), thus avoiding problematic business termination or sole proprietor death.

- **Much less administrative paperwork and record-keeping**— For example, it's *usually* easier to form an LLC than one of the other forms of business entities.

Disadvantages of LLCs

While a limited liability company (LLC) offers many advantages over other types of business entities, there are also some disadvantages:

- Earnings of most members of an LLC are generally subject to self-employment tax.

- Many investors are not as comfortable investing in LLCs.

- Some states do not tax partnerships but will tax limited liability companies.

Subchapter S-Corporation

S-corporations, or S-corps, are corporations that generally don't pay taxes directly. Instead, all the income, deductions, and other tax items are passed on to the shareholders of the corporation. They are known as *flow-through* or *pass-through* entities because income, losses, and deductions pass through to the individual owners. The S-corp was established by Congress to give small businesses the flexibility of limited liability protection and ease of entity creation. The shareholders of S-corps report the S-corp's income, losses, and deductions on their personal tax returns via Schedule K-1 and pay taxes at their individual income tax rates.

Major benefit of an S-corp

There isn't the issue of double taxation that the shareholders of a C-corp will experience. For example, a C-corp generally pays taxes on profit it earns. After which the C-corp may decide to give the shareholders a share of the C-corp's profits via a dividend. The shareholder of a C-corp is also required to pay taxes on the dividend he or she received from the C-corp—in effect he or she is paying taxes twice on the same income. The S-corp eliminates the concept of double taxation by allowing the shareholders of the S-corp to only pay taxes on their share in the S-corp.

To qualify for S-corporation status, the corporation must meet the following requirements:

- The company must be a domestic corporation.
- Shareholders must be U.S. citizens or permanent resident aliens.
- S-corps cannot have more than 100 shareholders.
- S-corps can only have one class of stock.
- Certain financial institutions, insurance companies, and domestic international sales corporations are ineligible for S-corp status.
- Profits and losses *must* be allocated according to the ownership shares or percentages of the individual owners.

The S-corp rules are relatively strict; not adhering to them explicitly will revoke your S-corp election with the IRS. You don't want that! Consult a CPA if you have specific questions.

Sole Proprietorship

A sole proprietorship is a business entity that has only one owner. The owner doesn't create an entity but operates the business using a "Doing Business As" (DBA) designation filed in the state he or she lives in. The owner is generally liable and responsible for all the debts incurred by the business and receives all the profits and losses as well. This is one of the least desired structures in my opinion because a sole proprietorship offers no legal and liability protection in the event a legal problem arises.

Partnership

A partnership is a legal entity comprised of two or more people coming together to operate a business. Partners contribute money, time, experience, or property in exchange for an ownership percentage in the partnership. Small-business and finance expert Dave Ramsey often says, "The only ship that won't sail is a partnership!" This greatly illustrates the need for a well-prepared and well-executed partnership agreement.

Many people will say at this juncture: "But my partner is one of my best friends, and we've never fought over money before!" There's a first time for everything, but more importantly, what happens if one of you decides to not work as hard? The lazy partner is still entitled to a share of profits produced by the other's hard work. You can change that by having a strong partnership agreement that has been executed by a licensed attorney. Here are a few more important caveats regarding partnership agreements:

- Each partner should have his own attorney in order to ensure everyone's best interests are accounted for.

- Make sure your partnership agreement has specific responsibilities for each partner.

- Never make the partnership 50/50 if there are only two partners. There should always be a slight majority.

- Make sure the partnership agreement has a specific process should the partnership encounter problems or fail altogether.

Entity Comparison Chart

	Limited Liability Company (LLC)	S- Corporation	C Corporation	Sole Proprietorship	Partnership
Ease of Filing	Yes	Yes	No	N/A	No
Cost of filing	Low	Low	Low	N/A	Low
Limited Liability	Yes	Yes	Yes	No	Yes
Pass-through of taxes	Yes	Yes	No	N/A	Yes
Limitation on number of owners	No	Yes	No	Yes	No

What Entity Is Best For Me?

This isn't an easy question to answer. Make sure you speak with an attorney and/or a CPA because everyone's facts and circumstances are different. The type of entity you select will depend on the type of business you're starting as well as what you plan on doing in the future. If you're a sole owner and operate as a service provider or sell products, an LLC may be a great way to start. Also, C-corps require annual meetings and corporate formalities that are not required for LLCs. Any losses you generate are generally carried to your personal tax return but it's important you operate like a business because of the IRS Hobby Loss Rules. (More on these pesky rules in the next chapter.)

Forming a Legal Entity

It was a nightmare to form a business entity before the Internet. The good news is that there are now a variety of companies online that can help you file your incorporation papers. Some of the most frequent questions I receive are about the nuances and processes of filing a legal entity as economically as possible.

I have experience with the two leaders in business filing and incorporation services—Legal Zoom and CorpNet. I recently interviewed the founder of CorpNet for a simple process for forming a business entity. I've personally formed entities in the past and I've become familiar with CorpNet's services as a result. This is the general process and step-by-step guide for forming a business entity for your business. This can all be done online.

1. Choose a business name: The first step is to ensure that your business name is available and that someone else isn't already using it. Using CorpNet.com's home page as an example, simply click on **Free Business Name Search** to get started. Their search tool is completely free and you'll know within a day if your proposed name is available in your state. There's a similar process on Legal Zoom.

2. Choose a business structure: Choosing a business structure (LLC, C-corporation, S-corporation, sole proprietorship, or partnership) is an important step that should not be taken lightly, because your choice will impact how you run your company. If you're not sure

which business structure is right for you, use CorpNet.com's free Business Structure Wizard. It will guide you through a series of questions and then propose a business structure based on your answers. In addition, you should speak with your CPA or attorney to make sure all your needs are met.

3. Select your state of registration: After you complete the business structure wizard, you can get started right from the results page. Choose your state of registration and click **Get Started**. Not sure which state to choose? As a general guideline, if your business will have five shareholders or fewer, it's going to be simplest and most affordable to select the state where you live or will have an office.

4. Select your registration package: CorpNet.com offers three formation packages for incorporating a business or forming an LLC: Basic, Deluxe, and Complete. The chart on the order form outlines exactly what you get from each level.

5. Select your filing speed: Depending on your sense of urgency, you can choose standard, express, or even 24-hour processing (not available in all states). The order form will show you exactly how much each service costs and how quickly you'll get your registration for your particular state. After you've selected your package and speed, click on **Start Order** on the right side of the page to continue the process.

6. Fill out the one-page Incorporation/LLC questionnaire: You'll be asked basic questions such as your contact name, the name and address of the business you're starting, the registered agent information (who will act as the agent of the corporation or LLC), director and officer information (for a Corporation), and so on. In most cases, this page can be filled out in about three minutes, but you can call CorpNet if you have any questions. Once your details are entered, submit the payment, and CorpNet will take care of the rest.

7. Obtain an EIN (employer information number): Think of an EIN as a social security number for your business; it's how the IRS keeps track of your business, and you need one to open a business bank account. If you selected CorpNet's Deluxe or Complete package, they'll automatically get an EIN for you. If you selected a Basic package, you'll need to go to the IRS Website to get your EIN.

8. Obtain any necessary business licenses, permits, or DBAs:
Depending on your business type and where you live, you may need
to get a business license or permit from your state, county, or town.
Check with your county office or state's secretary of state office to
find out what you need. Also, if you plan on conducting business
under a different name than what you registered as (for example,
CorpNet vs. CorpNet.com), you'll need to file a DBA to use the
other name. You can file a DBA with CorpNet (from the home page,
click on **Business Filings, Doing Business As—File a DBA**).

9. Set up a business bank account: As an LLC or corporation, you'll
need to keep your business finances separate from your personal
finances. Once you have your corporation/LLC certificate and your
EIN, go to a bank and set up your business account.

10. Keep your business in compliance: Your legal obligations don't end
once you've set up your business; you need to make sure it stays in
good standing by keeping up with your taxes, sending in an annual
report to the state, and numerous other duties. You can sign up
for the CorpNet's free B.I.Z tool. It's like a personal compliance
concierge service that will automatically send you reminders
whenever there's an important deadline coming up.

■■■

Now that we've covered how to select your business entity, in the next
chapter we'll go over some of the tax issues you're likely to encounter as a
new small-business owner.

Chapter 11
Tax Issues

The IRS has rules for business losses because business owners have the opportunity to use losses on their personal tax returns. For example, LLCs and S-corps allow for losses generated by your business to be applied to your personal tax return. This is also known as the *pass-through* of tax items. The problem with this loophole is that people would create companies and generate losses by those companies. The losses would then flow to the owner's individual tax return, lowering his or her income taxes. The IRS put a stop to that practice by creating and enforcing Section 183 of the Internal Revenue Code (IRC).

Are You Engaged in a For-Profit Endeavor?

Internal Revenue Code Section 183 (Activities Not Engaged in for Profit) limits deductions that can be claimed when an activity is not engaged in for profit. IRC 183 is sometimes referred to as the Hobby Loss Rule. In general, you can deduct expenses that are both necessary and ordinary in running your business. Those are your regular expenses, provided that you are engaged in a business for profit.

The IRS provides an educational fact sheet (FS-2008-23, June 2008) that provides information for determining if your business qualifies as an "activity engaged in for profit" and what deductions are limited if your business doesn't qualify. Is your hobby really an activity engaged in for profit? The following factors, though not all inclusive, may help you to determine whether your activity is an activity engaged in for profit or just a hobby:

- Does the time and effort put into the activity indicate an intention to make a profit?
- Do you depend on income from the activity?
- If there are losses, are they due to circumstances beyond your control or did they occur in the start-up phase of the business?

- Have you changed methods of operation to improve profitability?

- Do you have the knowledge needed to carry on the activity as a successful business?

- Have you made a profit in similar activities in the past?

- Does the activity make a profit in some years?

- Do you expect to make a profit in the future from the appreciation of assets used in the activity?

The IRS will consider your business as engaged in for profit if you make profit in at least three out of the last five years, including the current year. If an activity is not for profit, losses from that activity may not be used to offset other income. An activity produces a loss when related expenses exceed income. The limit on not-for-profit losses applies to individuals, partnerships, estates, trusts, and S-corporations. It does not apply to corporations other than S-corporations.

What are allowable hobby deductions under IRC 183? If your activity is not carried on for profit, allowable deductions cannot exceed the gross receipts for the activity. Deductions for hobby activities are claimed as itemized deductions on Schedule A, Form 1040. These deductions must be taken in the following order and only to the extent stated in each of three categories:

1. Deductions that a taxpayer may claim for certain personal expenses, such as home mortgage interest and taxes, may be taken in full.

2. Deductions that don't result in an adjustment to the basis of property, such as advertising, insurance premiums, and wages, may be taken next, to the extent gross income for the activity is more than the deductions from the first category.

3. Deductions that reduce the basis of property, such as depreciation and amortization, are taken last, but only to the extent gross income for the activity is more than the deductions taken in the first two categories.

IRS Audits

Taxes are the one area where brave people suddenly become scared. The misconception is that the IRS is out to get the average taxpaying and government-fearing American. The reality is the IRS uses software programs and other tools to randomly select taxpayers to review and/or audit. A large part of my background as a CPA includes experiences in tax and dealing with the IRS. I've spent a lot of time defending small businesses and taxpayers before the IRS and have helped to negotiate settlements for my clients. As a result, I was able to learn from my experiences and provide insights for people who ask.

The thought of receiving a letter from the IRS can cause your blood pressure to rise and give you a tremendous amount of stress. More often than not, a letter from the IRS is merely a letter of inquiry about particular tax items—for example, revenue or income, and expenses or deductions. It's important to understand what the IRS is asking you to do. The IRS may ask you in the initial letter to provide additional documentation for revenues or expenses you listed on your tax return. The initial letter of inquiry can sometimes be resolved simply by answering their questions.

The IRS sent me a letter of inquiry a year after I started my clothing line. They wanted to review some of the expenses I had deducted on my tax return. I was initially startled, but then I remembered that the request was customary and pretty routine. I had a record of all my expenses because I had used an American Express charge card for purchases. The key is to not panic and reach out to a licensed professional who is authorized to speak to the IRS on your behalf. This professional could be a CPA, a licensed attorney, or an enrolled agent.

CPA

Certified public accountant, or CPA, is the title given to qualified accountants who have passed a standard CPA examination. Qualified applicants are required to have a variety accounting classes and relevant work experience under their belts in order to take the CPA exam. People who have passed the CPA exam are required to take continuing professional education courses in order to keep their license current.

Attorney

An attorney is someone who has attended law school and passed the Bar exam after graduation. Attorneys are required to be licensed in the states in which they practice law. More importantly, as you can for CPAs, you can search the state's certification database for the status of a lawyer's right to practice law in that state.

Enrolled Agent

Enrolled means "licensed to practice by the federal government," and *agent* means "authorized to appear in the place of the taxpayer before the IRS." Only enrolled agents, attorneys, and CPAs have unlimited rights to represent taxpayers before the IRS. The license is earned in one of two ways: by passing a comprehensive examination which covers all aspects of the tax code, or having worked at the IRS for five years in a position that regularly interpreted and applied the tax code and its regulations.

Potential Audit Triggers

According to the IRS's Website and other publications, there are several frequently asked questions about tax audits for the self-employed and small businesses. (Source: *www.irs.gov/Businesses/Small-Businesses-%26-Self-Employed/IRS-Audit-FAQs#keypoint3.*) When returns are filed, they are compared against norms for similar returns. The norms are developed from audits of a statistically valid random sample of returns. These returns are selected as part of the national research program the IRS conducts to update return selection information.

Meanwhile, the IRS assigns numerical weights to certain tax return characteristics. These weights are added together to obtain a national composite score for all tax returns. When the total score of all selected items on your tax return exceeds the national average score set by the IRS, the agency will flag the return for a possible audit. The exact items the IRS zeroes in on and scoring method is a closely guarded secret, but some of the things the agency is believed to scrutinize include:

- Large amounts of income not subject to tax withholding.
- Unusually large amounts of deductions claimed than seem reasonable when compared to your income.
- A large number of dependent exemptions claimed that does not agree with reported social security numbers (SSNs).
- Large deductions for charitable contributions, casualty losses, home office expenses, and travel and entertainment expenses.
- A change of address when not reporting a sale of your residence and not changing your home related deductions.
- Running a cash-only business.
- Deducting business losses (Hobby Loss).

While an IRS audit is not something most sane folks want to go through, it also isn't necessarily something to be feared. If you have kept complete and accurate records of all of your deductions and have reported all of your income, you should be fine. In fact, in about a quarter of audits, the IRS makes no changes or actually issues a refund.

■■■

Now that we've gotten that uncomfortable but necessary section over with, we can move on to creating a strategy for your new business!

Chapter 12

The Four S's: Strategy (Pricing)

A friend of mine, Sarah, started a new gluten-free cupcake business. Her friends and family love the taste of the cupcakes and now her church wants to order three dozen. She wanted to know how much she should charge her customers. I told Sarah that the short answer is "It depends." I then went on to explain why it depends—which is what I'll do later in this chapter. This area, pricing, by far is one of the biggest obstacles entrepreneurs face. Pricing is important because you will lose money on every sale if you price too low. If you price too high, you can lose potential sales in the process, especially if you're a new business. It's extremely difficult to succeed if you start a handbag company and set your pricing at $2,000 per bag, particularly if there isn't any inherent value in it yet. Many customers realize that they can buy a more established brand for the same price or lower. If you price your handbag at $200 but it costs $300 to produce, you'll lose $100 for each bag you sell. In this scenario, it's actually better to not sell handbags at all and just close the business.

One size does not fit all, and this applies to your business, as well. Your pricing should depend on the nature of your business. Pricing isn't just an arbitrary number, even though many entrepreneurs treat it that way. The businesses that can evaluate the best pricing levels will do well regardless of the economy. In other words, you have to know why you could and should charge a certain price. It's important to understand the three most important pricing theories a small business should consider in order to maximize your pricing ability and make the most money from each sale.

There are three major pricing theories that all entrepreneurs and small-business owners should understand before they start their business; otherwise, their entrepreneurial experience will be short-lived. These theories are:

1. Competition or competitive pricing.
2. Cost pricing.
3. Value pricing.

Competition Pricing

Competition or competitive pricing is a pricing method in which a business sets price based on its competitors. This is generally done when there's an established market leader for products or services, and competitors set their prices according to the market leader. Here's an example: Best Buy has a Samsung 40-inch, LCD television for sale for $500. A new upstart company named Hamstrung could offer a 40-inch LCD TV for $300, provided its customers are sensitive to price. Hamstrung's strategy is to charge less than what the market leader is. This pricing strategy is easier when dealing with products that are being bought and resold—a wholesaler, for example. The problem is setting your prices according to your competitors can create an anchor of quality. Your customers begin to perceive you as a lower quality version of the highest-priced product. Lower price equals lower quality equals not interested! As a customer, you're probably thinking, *Why does this television cost $200 less than a Samsung?* If you're familiar with Samsung you're aware of the quality of their products. Unfortunately for Hamstrung, they have now inadvertently told customers that their products are inferior to those of Samsung.

Many small-business owners automatically default to this theory without thinking. When discussing their prices, you'll often hear things like, "We're cheaper than our competitors!" or "Nobody beats our prices! Bring in a competitor's coupon and we'll match it!" But how can you base your prices on your competitors if you don't know their costs and expenses? It's a challenge to offer the same price even if it's a comparable product, because the cost of acquiring your products for inventory may differ based on the quantity acquired.

So, what if my competitors are established and there's no way I can compete with such low prices? I know of countless stories within the last 20 years of Wal-Mart superstores moving into towns and putting small mom-and-pop shops out of business. Most people thinks this happens because Wal-Mart prices are extremely low and other stores can't compete at the same level without going out of business. The reality is a lot of these companies eventually go out business for a variety of reasons, and pricing may be only a small piece of the failure puzzle.

Economies of Scale

One of the reasons I say never (or try never) to compete on price is the theory of *economies of scale*. Economies of scale are cost savings that companies receive because of their size. For example, Wal-Mart has the strength of a large organization, and efficiencies in operations and distribution advantages allow them to make and/or acquire products more cheaply than smaller companies can.

Economies of scale apply to a variety of organizational and business situations and at various levels, such as a business or manufacturing unit, plant or an entire company. For example, a large manufacturing facility would be expected to have a lower cost per unit of output than a smaller facility, all other factors being equal, while a company with many facilities should have a cost advantage over a competitor with fewer facilities. When you order products from a supplier they'll generally give you a discount for ordering more, because the increase of production makes the supplies cheaper.

In my experiences working with small businesses, I've seen owners price their products and services according to potential competitors but not comparable competitors. I conducted a quick survey of how small businesses priced their products and/or services across the United States. The bottom line is 85 percent of the businesses I surveyed used competition pricing as a strategy to set their prices. Chances are you probably do the same thing. Here are a few examples of businesses that embrace the concept of competitive pricing.

A company called Neon Tiki Tribe's main product is a book series for dyslexic children. The Neon Tiki Tribe teaches children how to handle real-life problems through fun, action-packed adventures. They determined their pricing structure by researching competitor's prices. According to the company, they also determined their pricing structure by putting together a sample group of targeted buyers that could help them determine the best price points for their books.

It's interesting what Neon Tiki Tribe did after setting a benchmark for pricing. They formed two sample groups of targeted buyers who would be interested in their product. They gave one sample group a survey with three choices to choose from of fixed prices that they felt would be best for a children's book. In the second sample group they asked potential buyers what price they would be willing to pay for their product. Neon Tiki Tribe then took an average of the results provided. The company also realized from their research that they had the ability to charge more for their products but opted not to do so because their main goal is to help as many dyslexic children as possible. They didn't want price to be the reason a boy or girl couldn't read one of their books. Their margins were still pretty good despite pricing their products lower than those of their competitors.

In another example, Hype Up Your Day, Inc., provides human resources development services to corporations. The company also designs human resources training packages to improve employee morale and productivity. It determined its pricing structure by getting feedback from several different keynote speakers and corporate trainers on how they price their services. The company follows their competitor's model for prices and range of services, but it added a competitive edge by lowering the cost. Unfortunately the company feels this practice is necessary because it makes their customers feel like they are getting the best price possible. It also feels that customers have a perceived value of its service in mind. In other words, the company's prices are high enough to give customers the perception of value while still remaining lower than those of its competitors.

Competition can work for certain businesses, provided the business provides superior value and realizes what its customers value. Competition pricing can also work if you can produce your products or services for as low a price as possible and cover your existing costs in the process.

A friend of mine named Tiffany started out as a bookkeeper for a small custom cabinet shop and worked for additional small companies as side jobs while pursuing an undergraduate degree. Tiffany realized that most companies needed financial and bookkeeping help after working for various small businesses. She also noticed that the CPA firms she had worked for during the past 10 years were struggling with providing adequate customer service and commitment to taking care of their clients. She wanted to offer a lower-cost solution for small businesses. After acquiring experience in the bookkeeping space, she decided to leave her job, take all of the small companies she did side work for, and make it a full-time business.

When Tiffany first started her company, Sapphire Booking, she chose a rate based on what she felt was reasonable for her to earn and not necessarily based on competition. She had little overhead and fixed costs because she didn't have an office of employees. She used competition pricing in her second year of business and called other bookkeeping companies in her area that offered similar services, for price quotes. After receiving price quotes from approximately five companies for each service, she compared them with the amount of time required to complete each the task. She also factored in other overhead costs, such as software costs, that were now required. She wanted to set her prices under the market rate because she felt it gave her a competitive advantage by keeping lower prices on comparable services.

Cost-Plus Pricing

Cost-plus pricing is a simple pricing strategy that businesses use to determine the prices of their goods and services based on the cost of the goods or services offered. In other words, a business figures out its costs and then adds a mark-up, or profit margin, on top of it. The sum of those two factors makes up the price. Businesses of all sizes usually use this simple pricing model as a guideline for arriving at sale prices that will allow the company to cover both the cost of the product and other ancillary costs associated with the production and sale of the products, and still make a reasonable profit. This pricing strategy works for calculating the price of goods, such as the cost of a meal in a cafe, or services, like those provided by a plumber.

Services

Service is one area that applies cost-plus pricing, especially those services provided to the government, both Federal and state, by large and small businesses. The government often buys a certain number of hours of work from contractors at a fixed price, plus a percentage for profit. I experienced this working for some of the largest public accounting firms, wherein the firms would charge an hourly rate based on the level and experience of the consultant. That rate consisted of fixed costs for salary, benefits, and so on, and a moderate mark-up for profit.

Products

Products tend to be a little easier to determine pricing for. In cost-plus pricing, a company first determines its break-even price for the product. This is done by calculating all the costs involved in the production, marketing, and distribution of the product. Then, a mark-up is set for each unit based on the profit the company needs to make and the price it believes customers will pay. For example, if the company needs a 20-percent profit margin and the break-even price is $4.50, the price will be set at $5.40 ($4.50 ×1.20).

Lenny Kharitonov is the president of the Unlimited Furniture Group in the New York City area. The group operates the online furniture retailer Bedroomfurniturediscounts.com in addition to a brick-and-mortar store. Lenny is also on the board of directors for the Metropolitan Furnishings Association, an industry trade group. Lenny uses his 15 years of furniture retailing experience to develop, test, and implement pricing strategies that work for his businesses.

Lenny implemented a variety of cost-plus pricing strategies after testing them out with customers. He took an item's cost and calculated the mark-up required to cover the cost (the break-even) and make a reasonable profit. Some of his pricing is specified by certain vendors, as they are contractually required to sell at a certain price. As a result, the profit margins on those particular items aren't elastic or movable. The company has an interesting way to get customers back using price segmentation. For example, if a potential customer visits the Website and starts to make a purchase but ends up not checking out, the company will offer the customer a special promotion to give him/her another shot.

Disadvantages of Cost-Plus Pricing

Cost-plus pricing does not take into account the price of competing products. If your competitor charges less for a similar product, this pricing strategy may not work. You would have to either find a way to lower the costs for each product or accept a lower profit margin. Cost-plus pricing also does not account for the value a customer may have in the product. For example, your buyers may be willing to pay more for some of your products. A cost-plus strategy may not be responsive to changes in the market and can actually be an obstacle to long-term success.

Another drawback is that many small-business entrepreneurs fail to account for all their costs of production. I recently spoke with a woman who wanted to bake and sell bourbon cake balls to customers. She was having an issue determining the price to charge for a set. The bigger issue was that she was not accounting for her true costs, which included her time, packaging, Website(s), and other costs of running her business. The solution we used was to track her costs from the ingredients used, the time she spent baking, the packaging, and everything else. We then assigned the costs to each package produced and figured out what profit percentage was acceptable to her.

Value Pricing

People generally spend money for one reason: to solve a problem. There's almost always an underlying problem that the most successful businesses are capable of addressing and alleviating in subtle or not-so-subtle ways. Every time we make a purchase, we seek to solve a problem, whether we realize that or not. The goal is to differentiate your solutions from those of other businesses in the market place. Think of someone you know—anyone. If you think about what he or she likes spending money on, underneath that behavior will usually be a problem or pain point. This is exactly how you should consider targeting your clients and customers. What problems do they have that you can solve? Would-be entrepreneurs who want to start a business need to realize that it is not about starting a business; it's about the freedom to go out and help others and make money in the process.

If you focus on helping your customers solve their problems, they will be happier and more inclined to pay you money. Money will not be the issue. In other words, there is a direct relationship between solving a problem and the value received by your customer. Your customer won't nickel-and-dime you about how high your prices are. For example, if I charged a customer $1,000-plus but helped him start a business which then allowed him to successfully earn $10,000 per month, would it be worth it to that customer? Most definitely!

Value-based pricing is a pricing strategy that sets pricing for a product or a service on the perceived value the customer receives. Contrast this with cost-plus pricing, in which the price is based on the cost of the product or service provided to the customer plus a reasonable mark-up or profit margin. In value-based pricing, a company can charge a higher price on products or services provided there is a distinguishable benefit to what they offer. Competition pricing, on the other hand, forces you to anchor your price and quality to a market leader. More importantly, competition pricing tends to bring the "bottom feeders"—clients or customers who waste your time nickel-and-diming you because they don't value the service you provide.

Like many entrepreneurs, Karla Trotman has an undergraduate degree in business logistics with a minor in the legal environment of business. In addition, she worked for 10 years at leading retail companies in the areas of supply-chain logistics, distribution, and production scheduling. Her grandmother owned and operated a successful restaurant for more than 15 years. Karla's father currently owns an electronics manufacturing and engineering firm, which has been in business for more than 27 years. It's safe to say that entrepreneurship is in her blood. Her vast experience in the industry gave her the background she needed to develop pricing strategies.

After becoming pregnant and experiencing the normal difficulties of pregnancy, such as morning sickness and back pain, she realized that there were a slew of products that helped women deal with the discomfort that often went along with being pregnant. She used her background and degree to source the products that ultimately helped her though her pregnancy. As she did her research, she found that many of the inventors of these products didn't have the ability to mass distribute and market them. That is when she saw that the niche had been ignored. She not only gave birth to her child, but she also gave birth to Bellybuttonboutique.com, an online boutique that offers products of comfort, healing, and support to pre- and postnatal women.

Karla carved out a specific niche by focusing on women who are uncomfortable during pregnancy, which allows for price flexibility. Most of the products in her online boutique are bought wholesale and have a manufacturer's suggested retail price, or MSRP. A few other items require negotiating with the manufacturer to determine prices. In the event of a price increase, Karla mentions any product improvements in the product descriptions. In addition, she realizes that the value her online boutique offers allow for price flexibility provided the increase is only incremental. She also started using newsletters to keep her past customers and potential customers abreast of anything that may impact future sales—including price increases.

Karla initially believed that her online store needed to compete with lower-priced retailers like Amazon.com because she felt her customers were very price sensitive. She quickly realized that her ideal customer cares more about solving a problem and receiving quality products than price. Her customer is also more of a long-term client who focuses on value and the user experience. The woman shopping on Amazon.com for the cheapest prices isn't her ideal client because when you just want one thing, you head to Amazon; when you want a problem-solving product and great user experience, you go to a store that can customize your needs. As contrasted with competition or cost-plus pricing, it's a lot easier to build a business where the customer understands, appreciates, and pays you for that.

Never Compete on Price

Unless you're Wal-Mart and have the distribution, process, and procedures in place, you'll most likely lose your business if you compete on price. Your business will only be a number on a proposal page if price is the only differentiator between you and your next competitor. You have become a commodity in your marketplace. A commodity is a term used to describe a class of goods or services where there is demand, but no specific and qualitative difference between the suppliers in the market. For example, if I hired both Company A and Company B to paint the interiors of two rooms in my house, I probably wouldn't be able to tell the difference between the two companies in terms of their work. Being a commodity means your customers cannot tell who provided them with goods or services. That is a horrible position to put your company in. Your customers will then see you as replaceable, and you will eventually be replaced. Too many new business owners and entrepreneurs choose to put their business in this position, and that accelerates their failure.

Let's say you own a restaurant in a great neighborhood. In the middle of the night your water pipes burst. You call plumbers in the area at 2 a.m. and none of them offer emergency services. You eventually find a plumbing company called Randy & Sons that charges $500 to shut off the water and repair the break. At that point in time, you're not worried about price because the bigger problem is the flooding in your restaurant. You're not going to take the time to call 20 plumbers and compare all their prices. All the plumbers in the phone book offer plumbing services, but the one you end up hiring (Randy & Sons) offers emergency services. Randy & Sons differentiated themselves from their competitors and provided an additional and distinguishable benefit that was reflected in their prices. Are *you* providing additional value that can't be quantified? More importantly, are you making your customers aware of the additional benefits they receive by working with you?

Here's another example: A company that sells basic, white, 100-percent cotton athletic shirts would most likely use cost-plus pricing, because its product does not have any special features. It is probably manufactured overseas and is rather inexpensive to produce. However, what if your company sold sweat-wicking, extra-absorbent athletic shirts? You could use a variation of value-based pricing and sell its shirts at a higher price, because it provides something unique and valuable to athletic consumers. Can you put a price on or quantify the additional benefit of sweat-wicking fabric? If you are a person who sweats profusely, you will probably be open to paying more for the shirts because you have a problem that you need solved.

Narrow your business focus and establish a niche for your products or services. If you do this, you can identify what your smaller target market values and wants. Using Karla as an example, here's how:

1. **Establish your story:** It's important to be able to relate to your target market either through personal experiences or anecdotes. Karla experienced the difficulties of pregnancy firsthand when she had her first child.

2. **Identify the unique problems:** After speaking to other pregnant women, Karla realized that the majority of them experienced similar discomfort and were seeking solutions to a myriad of issues. Through her research, Karla also found that there were many products that alleviated those problems but getting access to these products proved difficult.

3. **Provide a value added solution:** Bellybuttonboutique.com provides an online marketplace for expecting mothers to find a myriad of products to deal with the difficulties of pregnancies.

Do you see why I'm an advocate for value-based pricing? Competing on price is difficult when you're first starting out. Actually, it is damn near impossible to compete as a newcomer with more established brands or competitors. Economies of scale and brand awareness are the major reasons. The businesses that try to compete on price usually do not last long and quickly go out of business.

I can hear you now: "That's great, Ebong, but what if I provide PR services for clients, and there are 3,000 public relations professionals in my area?" The short answer is, maybe you should quit if you want to be the 3,001st public-relations professional. The better answer is that you need to evaluate what, specifically, your unique talent is and determine whom you are currently serving. The additional value you bring may come from your personal and professional relationships. Do you know the right people who could help your clients? Can you write and craft press releases that get better results? Can you add tips or pointers on media training for your clients? Could you create a media workshop for small businesses that do not have the budget to hire you at your full rate but who might be open to a lower-priced workshop? Could you then make up the difference having 10 small businesses paying $2,000 for a one-day workshop?

I realize that I am harping on the importance of value-based pricing but this is an important strategy that will keep you from entering the pit of competition pricing. Value-based pricing forces you to evaluate your skills and the quality of your products and services. If you do so, you will start acquiring customers who want their problems solved and who are not as worried about saving 10 percent on your products because your competitors are cheaper.

Nothing is more confusing than the current healthcare system and the prices that are charged for medical services. There are several reasons why most people don't do price-comparison shopping for healthcare services and products. The first and obvious reason is that many people have insurance that pays for most or all of those services. The other reason is we see enormous value in curing or fixing whatever ails us. In other words, saving money is not as important if we die on an operating table trying to save money. It's virtually impossible to put a price on our health, and many choose not to. That said, finding a better product that surpasses the current method(s) of alleviating a chronic illness is something we'll find value in, as well—if the price is right!

Dr. Amy Baxter is the inventor of a curious but amazing little product called Buzzy for Shots. The Buzzy resembles a small vibrating bee that also contains a small ice pack. Using natural pain relief, Buzzy desensitizes the body's nerves, thereby dulling or eliminating sharp injection pain. In the same way that rubbing a bumped elbow helps, or cool running water soothes a burn, the Buzzy crowds out pain by sending stronger motion and temperature sensations down the nerves instead.

Dr. Baxter had initially struggled with her pricing strategy but eventually implemented a value-based pricing approach. She was initially charging $34.95 for the product plus shipping and handling. She subsequently shifted to a "free shipping" model and increased the price of the product to $39.95. Dr. Baxter's business increased as a result of the price increase, because her customers liked free shipping, even though the sticker price had increased. In this case, $34.95 versus $39.95 is not substantially or emotionally different. However, the free shipping added a distinguishable value to the product after the decision to purchase was already made. According to Dr. Baxter, people getting shots daily, particularly painful shots, routinely say that Buzzy is "worth its weight in gold, literally," or, at a minimum, "the best $40 they have ever spent." Dr. Baxter's product is unique and provides specific benefit to her customers. More importantly, there is no current direct competitor in that space nor are any other comparable products out there right now.

So how do you implement a strong value-based pricing model when there is already an established market leader? The key is to differentiate your business from the market leader by learning specifically what your customers need and want and then providing it to them with superior customer service. It's that simple!

Steps to Determine Your Pricing

Products

In pricing your product(s), you have to know how much it costs to make or buy it. Although this may sound intuitively obvious, too many people fail to figure out what their real product costs are and how much they should sell their products for. That greatly accelerates the rate of failure.

If you make a product, here are the steps to determine pricing:

1. Account for the cost of all of the materials used to make your product. For example, if you make and sell pies, you should track the portion of total ingredients needed to make one pie. If a one-pound bag of flour that costs $4.00 can produce 10 pie crusts, each pie crust costs $.40 worth of flour to make. Do the same thing with each ingredient. It can be cumbersome but if you don't know the true cost of ingredients per item, you will never grow your business.

2. Account for the amount of time it takes for you to create the product. Many entrepreneurs do not account for their time in determining their prices. This is an all-too-easy mistake to make, as many people don't see their time as having an absolute value.

3. The price of the product needs to be higher than what you make it for; otherwise you will lose money.

4. Look at competitors in your area, but always remember that part of your mission is to provide a value that is different from those of your competitors. If you are making pies, that differentiator can be different flavors, shapes, and sizes, and the service you provide to your customers.

If you resell a product, here are the steps to determine pricing:

1. This is a little easier, because the manufacturer generally sets the price of the product you purchase for resell—also known as the manufacturer's suggested retail price, or MSRP.

2. Competition pricing can play a role in your pricing if you are selling a product. You can determine the profit or mark-up that you want to earn on top of the MSRP.

Services

Services are a little more challenging to price because many entrepreneurs fail to account for the value of their time. This is why focusing on a niche and target market can make the difference between success and failure. By focusing on a niche and solving the problems of your customers, you alleviate their pain, which is a bigger concern to them than their money.

If you have ever tried to form a company you might have heard of CorpNet. The CEO of CorpNet, Inc., Nellie Akalp, is an entrepreneur, wife, and mother. She's been in the document filing industry since 1997. Drawing on her experience, she formed her first company based out of her living room. Working days and nights eventually paid off: In 2005 her company was acquired by Intuit; and later, in 2009, she and her business partners launched Corpnet.com after her non-compete agreement expired.

Pricing can be a problem for many small-business owners; however, Nellie was able to use her past experiences to determine the best pricing model for her services. She conducted a competitor analysis in her market and compared her findings to the needs of customers. Competition-based pricing can be useful when market leaders exist. Her sales originate from the company's Website and inbound calls, which gives CorpNet the ability to add value to their service offering when speaking to customers. Again, raising prices is possible if the customer experiences tremendous value.

In order to determine her prices, Nellie and her team researched the market and the consumers' needs. CorpNet conducted a competitor analysis to create a model that best served the clients' needs while still enabling the company to remain profitable. After this, raising prices became easier for them.

Mary Moore is the owner of both Green Clean Homes and Aloha Pet Sitting & Dog Walking in Gainesville, Florida. She created prices for her businesses by researching the other businesses in the area. She chose an average price for services after learning the prices and services of her competition. Through research, Mary realized that not being the cheapest or the most expensive was the best way to establish her services or products prices because offering low prices can give your customers an impression of poor quality.

In Mary's experience, earning awards, receiving certificates, and belonging to a professional association added value to her services. More importantly, these things gave Mary the opportunity to consistently raise prices. She found it easier to raise her prices by not notifying customers and simply giving them the increased price in subsequent orders.

There are a variety of ways to announce price increases to your customers. Many small-business owners struggle with setting prices in general, but they struggle even more with raising them. Mary tested two different ways to determine the best method for raising prices:

1. She formally notified the customers with letters about the price increases. She found that she lost a decent number of customers when she did this.

2. She just raised her prices without notifying customers of the increase. When she did this as part of the checkout process, most stayed on as customers. If her customers questioned the new price, the goodwill she had already established with them made it easier to justify the increase. This wasn't always the case, of course; her confidence to raise prices only came after developing unique experiences with her customers. Mary also candidly realized that the lack of confidence had an adverse effect on her pricing, her services, and the financial results of her business.

Mary's experiences aren't unique; many of you will have similar experiences. What if you have professional skills such as Web design, marketing, and bookkeeping and want to build a business offering your services to your niche market?

Pete Juratovic is the owner of a boutique Web design company called Clikzy.com, located in Alexandria, Virginia. Pricing in the Website design and branding field can vary dramatically between agencies. As a result, it's difficult to anchor prices for comparable services. A lot of new business owners cut their prices when they start, which makes it challenging for established agencies. Pete lost projects in the past because their price points were lower than those of his competitors, when the reality was that Clikzy could have done a better job and provided higher-quality solutions, solutions that would have saved the client thousands of dollars.

Pete frequently changes prices, but his company "price-projects" based on the customer's needs. There are primarily two kinds of clients in the Web design industry: the small-business owner, and the mid-level marketing manager. Clikzy's strategy is to offer a different approach for both of these types of clients. Small-business owners care most about getting the best value for their dollar. This is primarily because they feel the pain of the money leaving their wallet. In addition, small-business owners generally don't understand the importance of a high-performing Website. Mid-level marketing managers, on the other hand, care more about feeling comfortable with the team they are choosing. They do not care as much about a few thousand dollars because their company has a budget. They care more about the experience and a smooth process. It also helps to make this person look good to their coworkers and higher-ups.

In other words, knowing your customers and understanding what their underlying motivation or value needs are, will make it easier for you to increase your prices. The value received by your customers is directly related to the problem they want solved. Clikzy determines prices based on the client, the number of hours worked, previous work, and competitor analysis, but only with comparably sized companies and services.

By basing the project on the scope of work, Clikzy can raise prices because they proactively communicate with their clients in order to make them understand how much custom design work is required for their projects. In addition, Clikzy wants their clients to know how many different designs they may have to create for particular projects. The goal is for them to understand how much work an intangible product can entail. Despite their best efforts, some clients fail to understand why Clikzy would ever need to charge more, even if the company is re-quoting them for a redesign of their Website five years after the first Website was created.

What are you worth? You don't have to undercut your prices because you're starting a new business. Your pricing for services should be based on the amount of value you bring. For example, as a CPA, I generally charge clients between $300 and $400-plus per hour, depending on the services they need. Tax research services require a certain level of expertise that isn't common among other CPAs. More importantly, I have a diverse background that includes working with some of the largest global companies. My experiences warrant a higher fee. The bigger issue is making sure I solve problems for clients that differentiate myself from others and show clients that I am not a commodity.

If you're just starting out, find out what your competitors charge. Yes, you will be using competitor pricing, but only as a benchmark. Then, start raising your prices incrementally at consistent intervals during the next several months. You can only raise prices if your customers are experiencing increased value from your services.

On June 25, 2013, Starbucks raised its drink prices by approximately one percent across their stores nationwide. Starbucks has a consistent and targeted approach to raising prices based on the drinks and geographic locations of customers. All in all, less than a third of the total number of beverage prices were increased, and it did not have a large affect on customers. The truth is that Starbucks has been incrementally raising prices for the last 20 years. Every morning, customers line up for their lattes and frappucinos despite the rate increases. Starbucks has built a brand over decades that is about more than just coffee. It is an experience and symbol of superior service, culture, and products. The key is to emulate that vision when you start your business. Taking great care of your customers, listening to their particular needs, using your background, and solving their pain point or problems—all of this will allow you to raise your prices incrementally.

You can raise prices consistently when you bring extreme value to your customers by solving a big problem. Gary Vaynerchuk has been an entrepreneur his whole life. If you have ever heard his keynote speeches, you know that he loves to hustle! His story is no different than most other successful immigrant entrepreneurs. A man of infinitely many talents, he is best known as a social media guru, wine enthusiast, speaker, and best-selling author. His first major book, *Crush It—Why Now is the Time to Cash In on Your Passion,* was not only a *New York Times* best-seller, but it also served as a catalyst for thousands of entrepreneurs to leverage the power of the Internet. It would be an understatement to say Gary changed and improved my life in the world of social media. The book encourages people to determine what truly makes them happy and pursue monetizing it on the Internet. It argues that because of recent social and technological trends, the cost of producing content has been driven low enough that passion, knowledge, and effort (which he calls *sweat equity*), are now all one needs to build a brand and business. Gary's second book *The Thank You Economy* emphasizes the importance of authentic customer engagement via social media.

Gary consistently shares his passions for wine, entrepreneurship, and social engagement on his blogs, in his books, and in his speeches. I had the pleasure of interviewing Gary during my research for this book because I wanted to learn his insights into the world of pricing.

The concept of supply and demand is always at play in the world of business. Supply and demand is basically a subset of the value-versus-commodity concept: the more your customers value your service, the more you differentiate yourself from other competitors. Then you wouldn't be seen as a commodity because there is value that separates you from the average. Increased value means there is room for an increase in pricing. After all, at some point, someone decided that $150 for a haircut was acceptable!

Here are Gary's thoughts on pricing:

▶ Do your homework by performing a market analysis to determine the prices.

▶ Choose a price that makes sense for you and continue to raise them at consistent intervals (every six months, say) in order to gauge what is the highest price your customer will pay. Always ask your customers for more money because if you are solving their business problems, pricing won't be an issue.

(As a side note, Gary's new book *Jab, Jab, Jab, Right Hook* shows that while communication is still key, context matters more than ever. It's not just about developing high-quality content, but developing high-quality content perfectly adapted to specific social media platforms and mobile devices. Definitely worth the read!)

What Are You Worth?

Moshe Zusman, originally from Israel, is a photographer in Washington, DC who specializes in weddings, fashion, and other creative forms of photography. (He also took the photo on the cover of this book.) His story is truly fascinating and consistent with those of many successful immigrants. Moshe learned his trade by working under other established wedding photographers in Israel before immigrating to the United States.

Over the years, he developed a thriving business to the point that he is constantly booked. Moshe also teaches classes at the ART Institute on photography and on the business of being a photographer—including how photographers should price their services. I met with him to ask him how he would price his services for photography. This was his response:

> Many photographers think they are making money but they unfortunately don't account for all the costs they incur. For example, a photographer may charge $2,000 for wedding pictures over a five-hour period and think they are earning $400 per hour. What they fail to realize is they didn't account for the two years of school, the five extra hours spent retouching photos, and the extra time spent dealing with clients.

I wanted to drive home the importance of pricing strategy by citing examples of entrepreneurs from a wide variety of industries. There are several consistencies among them, whether you are established, like Gary Vaynerchuk and Nellie Akalp, or a relatively new entrepreneur, like Karla. Here is what you should do to create your pricing strategy:

1. Perform a competitive analysis of your industry and other businesses in your market to determine their prices.

2. Compare their prices and services to yours and increase yours by a little.

3. Think about how you can add value to your customers. How can you exceed the services you provide your customers and solve their problems in the process?

4. Continue to raise your prices every six months to determine the highest price your customers will pay.

5. (Note: this one is important!) Create three to four pricing packages to offer customers. This creates an "anchor and context" price which customers will use to compare and contrast. Have you ever notice that a lot of companies offer several pricing packages—for example, Bronze, Silver, Gold, and Platinum? Most people understand that the precious metals listed are in order of value, from Bronze, the lowest value, to Platinum, the highest value. This comparison gives the customer a feeling that each level of services you offer has a similar hierarchy, with Platinum level being the highest value package.

The other important issue comes from a human behavioral perspective. Customers tend to comparison shop for "context" if there are similar products and services. In other words, when customers buy, they judge their choices in terms of relative advantages they'll receive, not in terms of absolutes. You buy a product from a store; you don't look at the product and price tag and vote yes or no because you don't have the proper context. For example, let's say you're looking for someone to paint your house, and John Doe Painters quotes you a price of $1,500, informing you that they've given you a discount of $300. You don't know if that's a great price because there's no context to compare and contrast that price to. This explains why you would likely solicit bids from a few other painters to find what you believe to be the best price. People want to be able to compare to make sure that they're not spending more than they should. As a small-business owner, you should provide your customer with multiple pricing packages even if there are slight variations between them.

The key to contextual or anchor pricing is to offer related choices so that your customers feel comfortable making decisions about your product. Studies have shown that when given three choices, customers will most likely take the middle choice. So you should offer three related prices options, with the middle option being the option you want them to buy. Also, it's important to make sure the variations between price levels you offer the customer are easily comparable and what the customer actually cares about. For example, John Doe Painters offers house painting service for a discounted price of $1,200, which is their Platinum package.

Platinum Package—$1,200

Painting the walls of five rooms

Painting the baseboards and crown molding

Pre-painting coats (important for dark or stained walls)

High-quality paint

Gold Package—$900

Painting the walls of four rooms or fewer

Mid-quality paint

Silver Package—$650

Painting the walls of two rooms

Mid-quality paint

You have provided three options to your customer that offer slightly similar but different values of services. Because you've provided proper context and other options, your customer is probably thinking, *For $300 more, I get one more room, prep work, all moldings painted, and higher quality paint. That's worth it for me!*

There's a large psychological component to pricing and how customers buy goods and services. This area of inquiry (known as behavioral economics or finance) studies the effects of social, cognitive, and emotional factors on the economic decisions of individuals and institutions and the consequences for market prices, returns, and the resource allocation. Setting prices and marketing products to your customers are both sciences that have been studied over the years. The results of these studies, by experts such as Dan Ariely, Amos Tversky, Derek Halpern, and Ramit

Sethi, have been telling us that pricing matters. I strongly suggest you read and follow the blogs of Ariely, Halpern, and Sethi. Learning and implementing the concepts behind behavioral economics is imperative to the success of your business.

A well-known behavioral economics consumer pricing study by Amos Tversky and Itamar Simonson illustrates consumer behavior regarding price. A synopsis of the findings was addressed in an article written by Tversky in the *Journal of Marketing* in 1991. In the 1990s, high-end home ware retailer Williams-Sonoma offered a bread maker to customers for $275 after much consumer research. Sales of the bread maker were surprisingly horrible. Frustrated by the poor sales, management brought in a marketing research firm that recommended Williams-Sonoma introduce a slightly bigger, higher-quality bread maker at double the price point. As a result, Williams-Sonoma introduced a larger and better premium bread maker priced at $429. Almost immediately, sales of the lower priced bread maker of $275 took off, while sales of the premium bread maker had moderate sales.

There was no way for Williams-Sonoma (or consumers) to gauge the value of making your own bread at home because the original bread maker was a brand new product and concept in the marketplace. The basic problem was there wasn't a context in the price and the product for customers to compare. Customers couldn't understand if the $275 price point was actually attractive because there was nothing to compare it to. By introducing a slightly better product at a significantly higher price point, Williams-Sonoma provided the point of comparison for consumers that made the $275 seem like an attractive proposition and, more importantly, a "deal."

When you're launching a new product or service in the market, create multiple tiers or levels of pricing. If you don't provide options for your customers to compare the value of your products or services, they may not take the risk of buying from you. Create a tiered product strategy as Williams-Sonoma did, or try offering a discount for a longer commitment (for example, 25 percent off if you make a year-long commitment). Remember that people don't make decisions in a vacuum. Price your product in a way that takes advantage of that.

Chapter 13
Know Your Numbers

Hopefully it is now obvious that your pricing is one of the most important parts of building a successful business. Another important aspect of your business is your numbers. Just like the numbers that measure and quantify your health—heart rate, cholesterol, and blood pressure—there are similar numbers that will indicate the overall health of your business. You have to know your numbers—what they mean for your business and how they compare to industry standards.

Shark Tank is a reality show on ABC in which aspiring entrepreneurs present their businesses in front of five potential investors. These entrepreneurs have a limited amount of time to pitch their ideas and solicit an investment from one or more of the investors. One episode really highlights the importance of understanding and knowing your numbers. It also illustrates the need for this book as a training tool for small-business owners and start-ups.

Bea Arthur is the founder and CEO of Pretty Padded Room, an online marketplace that allows people to connect with trained therapists online to help them address their stress issues. Bea's presentation starts off well, and the Sharks are relatively interested in the concept and business model. Things go south, however, after the Sharks ask Bea about her business numbers, customary for a subscription-based business. After all the Sharks reject the opportunity to invest in Pretty Padded Room, Kevin O'Leary uses an apt metaphor to explain the mistakes Bea made in her presentation. There's a beach where large amounts of seal reside. The seals of this beach have a diet of tuna, which is plentiful in the sea. The seals also know that they can't go into the ocean because the ocean has a lot of sharks, which live on a diet of seals. All of the seals are starving on the beach. Days of not eating quickly turn into weeks, until the first seal, in a starvation delirium, goes into the water. That first seal is devoured by several sharks, which serves as a warning to all the other seals to not go into the water.

O'Leary proceeds to tell Bea that not knowing enough about her numbers will serve as a warning to all the other contestants to never make the same mistake.

Here are the numbers, or figures, you need to know for your business. Otherwise, you'll be the first seal to enter the ocean of sharks (that is, the marketplace) that will devour you and your business.

▶ **Working capital:** Working capital is the capital you have available to work with today. This is determined by subtracting current liabilities from current assets. A rule of thumb says you should have $1.50 to $2 of current assets for every $1 of current liabilities.

▶ **Revenues:** Know your sales on a monthly, quarterly, and year-to-date basis. Compare these to your plan to see if you are behind or ahead.

▶ **Gross profit:** Revenues less the direct costs of producing your product is your gross profit. In most cases, there should be 50 percent or more of your sales volume left over after you subtract your direct costs (cost of goods sold).

▶ **Profit margin:** Subtract the total of your general and administrative expenses from your gross profit, then divide that number by your sales. This number will tell you how profitable the business is. If the number is negative, you are losing money. Make sure the number is as good as or better than others in your industry. If the typical profit margin in your industry is 12 percent and yours is 5 percent, you are not managing your business as well as your competitors. Find out what you need to do to improve that margin.

▶ **Marketing expenses**: The largest marketing expense is often advertising. You should be able to turn up or slow down your sales by adjusting your advertising expenditures. If there does not appear to be a correlation between advertising and sales, then there may be something wrong with your advertising strategy. The important point is that if you do not compare your advertising expenses and sales, how will you know the effectiveness of your advertising?

The marketplace is going to go to the people and businesses that evolve. It's not going to go to those that are stuck in the past!

Chapter 14
Customer/Market Fit

Product market fit is a term used to describe the degree to which a product or a service has a market that is satisfied by that particular product or service. Is there a market that will pay for your product or service, and is that market large enough to sustain your business? There are plenty of products and services in the marketplace that don't solve problems. Remember, solving a problem is the major reason people spend money. If your product or service doesn't solve a problem, no one will care about it or buy it. You'll simply go out of business. That's really no different than throwing darts at a dartboard, hoping against hope that you'll hit the mark somehow. This is another reason why targeting a niche is so important. It is easier to determine what problem your niche or market wants solved.

This may sound obvious, but how many times have you had a friend share a start-up idea that doesn't solve a problem? Too many entrepreneurs focus on ideas that are new or that haven't yet been attempted. Remember that being the first with an idea is irrelevant, because if there isn't a market of consumers to buy your product or services, you will go out of business.

Here are a few methods to determine product market fit:

▶ Determine your niche (as we discussed before).

▶ Use social media tools to find out what problem people want solved.

▶ Get on Facebook. Solicit feedback from friends using a basic survey question about your product without mentioning your company or product.

▶ Use Twitter. Solicit feedback from your followers in the same way you did with Facebook. Then search for other Twitter followers that match similar keywords to your business. For example, if you're a Web designer, look for other Web designers on Twitter and ask them for their opinions. If your niche is small business, do a Twitter search for small businesses and ask them what problems they've come across with Web design.

▶ Get in on LinkedIn. LinkedIn is a great way to interact with other like-minded professionals. More importantly, LinkedIn is comprised of many small-business owners looking to grow their networks. Join LinkedIn professional groups for small-business and Web design.

▶ Use YouTube. As of this writing, YouTube is the second largest search engine out there. "How-to" videos are among the most popular offerings on YouTube. Millions of people search YouTube for how-to videos for almost every subject. I created a how-to video several years ago that taught you how to file your own Federal income tax extension form. The video has had thousands of views, and there is still a significant uptick in views every April 14. By reviewing the comments and questions, I can determine the needs of potential customers. In addition, these customers will eventually need to have their income tax return completed, which is something I can offer them later.

Chapter 15

The Four S's: Systems (Process)

Any task that requires repetition can be organized as a process. A business process is a series of steps and procedures that automate repetitive tasks. Why is this important? Humans exhibit habitual tendencies similar to those of animals from a physiological perspective. Being habitual creatures allows us to operate on autopilot so we can focus on other, more important aspects of life. We develop a rote method to do all of the tasks that are not necessarily important and don't require precision thinking. For example, we brush our teeth, comb our hair, and eat certain foods the same way every day. There are probably as many as 50 different repetitive tasks we do the same way every day, and we only notice the difference when circumstances change.

Several years ago I broke my right humerus bone, which is in the upper arm where the biceps and triceps muscles are located, in a basketball accident. I am right-handed so I use my right hand for almost everything. To say the experience of having to use my left hand for everything was trying would be an understatement. For 34 years, I had relied on my right hand to operate on autopilot and do everything that needed to be done without having to think or worry about it. After I broke my arm, I could no longer rely on that process and had to train my left hand to cope with the loss of efficiency and take up the slack.

Process in business (and the efficiency that goes with it) is just as important, and should be just as automatic, as my right-handedness. More than half of all businesses fail in their first year, and process, or lack thereof, often plays a vital role in their demise. Process and efficiency allow you to focus on the income-producing activities of your business, like acquiring new customers and servicing existing customers. Conversely, a lack of process will prohibit you from focusing on running and growing your business. We have all seen business owners who have their hands in every aspect of their business. They usually aren't very successful, nor do they last very long.

The Three P's

One of my favorite new reality television series is *The Profit* on CNBC. The show premiered in July of 2013 and is akin to a combination of Bravo Network's *Tabitha's Salon Takeovers*, Fox's *Gordon Ramsey's Kitchen Nightmares*, and ABC's *Shark Tank*. The show stars Camping World CEO and serial entrepreneur Marcus Lemonis. Lemonis shares the nuts and bolts of his $3 billion outdoor empire. Lemonis didn't get where he is today by just selling tents; rather, he makes an amazing living out of finding, acquiring, and turning around struggling companies.

Have you ever heard people say things like "It takes money to make money" and "He's lucky that his business is taking off"? The mistake people make is they believe the success of the rich is predicated on luck, opportunity, and tons of money. For Lemonis, the reality is that there is a time-tested formula to both his business acquisitions and his success. The formula is people, process, and product, also known as the Three P's.

It's obvious that people are important to the organization's ability to operate and get things done. It just makes sense. The people in a company have to be adequately 1) trained, 2) empowered, and 3) held accountable. The best companies in the world with the best products also have people who have bought into the company culture. Starbucks is a prime example of this. In a recent case study from the Core Values Institute, Shaun Frankson interviewed a former Starbucks employee for insights into the company's corporate culture. The former employee said Starbucks' culture had slightly deteriorated because management failed to lead by example. It is important to know this decline occurred during the time Howard Schultz was not at the helm of the company. The decline outlines the obvious point that culture comes from the head of the organization, and the head sets the tone. Why is that important? The culture you set for your business transcends management and employees, and rests in the customers' experiences. Crappy leadership leads to crappy employees leads to crappy customer experiences leads to crappy reputation leads to crappy sales. Starting to see a pattern here?

How did Schultz set the culture and tone for Starbucks? Schultz got Starbucks employees to buy into the goals and principles of the company. Because employees are customer-facing, customers' experiences become an extension of leadership. He implemented the "Starbucks Experience," which is comprised of two main parts: Partner Ethos and the Five Principles.

Process for Big Businesses: The Starbucks Experience

The Partner Ethos

- **Employees are partners:** Employees, also known as partners, are encouraged to actively participate in the company by contributing new ideas on improving products and growing business.

- **Leaders transmit the culture:** Schultz realizes that culture comes from the top. As a result, managers are responsible for relaying the Starbucks culture directly to employees. In addition, partners are extensively trained in the high standards of Starbucks' products and service.

The Five Principles

1. **"Make it your own":** Partners are encouraged to customize the experience for customers.

2. **"Everything matters":** Partners are encouraged to focus on every aspect of the job and to not lose sight of the customer's point of view.

3. **"Surprise and delight":** Make the coffee buying experience enjoyable for the customer by doing the unexpected.

4. **"Embrace resistance":** Starbucks encourages partners to be accountable and learn from their mistakes.

5. **"Leave your mark":** Do your job so that your customers remember you.

(Source: *http://corevaluesinstitute.ca/culture/starbucks-howard-schultz-culture-and-core-values/*)

Process for Small Businesses

Starbucks serves as a great example of the importance of process and systems, but I wanted to research how implementing a process in a small business affected the bottom line. The Pen Company (Thepencompany .com) is a family run online pen company with retail premises in the historic town of Hitchin, Hertfordshire, which is about 40 miles north of London. In speaking with ownership, I learned they had been implementing new processes for the past 12 months.

The company had been struggling with effectively communicating with their customers before implementing their new processes and a centralized project management system. In order to understand what processes needed to be implemented, the company conducted a survey with their existing customers to learn what areas were deficient. The survey highlighted that their customers wanted better communication regarding their orders. As a result, the company adopted the popular project management software called Basecamp (made by 37 Signals in Chicago, Illinois) to add structure to the project. Using a project management system also allowed them to improve how the company communicated internally. The company was able to do the following after three months:

- Introduce a new order update e-mailing system.
- Product reviews to see how customers found their service and product offerings.
- Develop a new basket system to make it easier for international customers.

Since the implementation of the new project management system, the company has reduced their order handling costs (for example, questions about products and billing) and increased their sales by more than 40 percent. By implementing certain processes, The Pen Company's five-member team is now able to grow their business internationally.

Content Harmony Agency

Content Harmony is a content marketing firm based out of Seattle. I spoke with Beth Anderson, who was the second employee to join the firm. One of Beth's first jobs was to create business procedures which at the time had been locked away in her boss's head. She created a variety of processes and procedures in order to automate repetitive tasks and responsibilities. For example:

- Steps for updating multi-page Websites for customers.
- "First Steps for New Employees," a guide to get new employees up to speed.
- Monthly reports for a variety of company metrics.

Determining whether to create a process or procedure was primarily Beth's decision, and she created processes for tasks she or a new employee was expected to repeat. According to Beth, the results have been good, and since hiring the company's third employee, she sees improvements in how general operations are conducted.

Chapter 16

Virtual Assistants and Interns

There are so many tasks to check off your list when starting a business. Unlike large corporations with hundreds of employees, you are your company's only employee. One of the biggest pitfalls for an entrepreneur is lack of time or productivity, because you wear all the hats! Remember the Staples commercial in which the business owner is the CEO, the executive assistant, the sales guy, *and* the IT department? The point of the commercial was to show that there is help available.

The Internet has made it easier for people to work remotely, and the virtual assistant industry has grown as a result. I regularly hire virtual assistants (VAs) to help me with writing articles, filling in client databases, and conducting online research. Your time is better served doing activities that directly yield money for your business. You should be spending time with clients and getting your first and second customer instead of entering business card information into Sugar CRM or a spreadsheet. Here are several virtual assistant services that I have used and recommend:

- Freelancer.com
- Zirtual.com (U.S.-based assistants only)
- Guru.com
- TaskRabbit.com (offers VAs that have undergone background checks)

The following are a few examples of the kinds of tasks you can outsource:

- Blogging and writing articles
- Creating e-mail marketing campaigns
- Searching for prospects online
- Appointment and meeting scheduling
- Doing online research

- Performing simple B=bookkeeping tasks
- Doing database entry
- Creating PowerPoint presentations

Hiring and Managing Virtual Assistants

Here are a few things you'll need to keep in mind when hiring and managing a VA:

▶ Ask for writing samples.

▶ Ask for references via the site (these sites tend to offer recommendations and feedback references).

▶ Ask for his or her commitment to a deadline.

▶ Offer a small bonus for beating the deadline if necessary.

▶ Hire someone who types proficiently.

▶ Ask for a fixed quote—if not possible, ask for a time budget.

▶ Look for someone who is proficient in Word, Excel, Access, e-mail, and so on.

▶ Ask the VA for milestones midway through projects to make sure he or she stays on task.

Chapter 17
Websites

I'm continually amazed at the quality of the Websites I see from new small-business owners. Websites were historically used as online calling cards or catalogues, but nowadays they are lot more than that. According to a January 2010 article by Carol Tice in *Entrepreneur Magazine*, approximately half of small businesses don't even have a Website. For the other half of small businesses that do, the quality tends to be pretty abysmal. So why the disparity? Many small businesses don't believe they need a Website, and according to Carol Tice, they are right. You don't need a Website if you don't want to be successful. But if you want to be successful, a Website is as important as having a name for your business. There isn't a successful company around that doesn't have one.

As of this writing, several companies offer free Websites, but there is an obvious trade-off for the free sites. For example, some free Website companies give you a free site but not your own URL. Several years ago companies offered free Websites using a blogging platform. Sites like Geocities and Blogspot provided a quick and easy way for people to get their Websites up and running without spending a lot of money. But the worst thing for your business would be to have a Website like *www.joeplumbing.blogspot.com* instead of *www.joeplumbing.com*; it's horrible from a branding perspective and not very professional. It gives the impression that your business is a hobby, something you're not all that committed to. Bottom line: if you don't have a decent Website, I will have serious doubts about your ability to provide high-quality services. Your customers will think the same way.

Fortunately, as the Internet landscape has become more sophisticated, it is easier and cheaper than ever to build a Website. Websites are really inexpensive these days, so there's no reason for your company not to have a good one.

Content Management Software

Rather than going the free route, using open-source CMS systems and finding someone to customize your site for you will give you a better long-term solution. Content management software (CMS) is software that allows you to easily create, change, and delete content on a Website without having to learn computer programming. The goal is to build a Website as economically as possible. Companies and entrepreneurs used to spend tens of thousands of dollars building complex Websites; not anymore. Websites can be built easily and for dramatically less using open-source software. Open-source software is software that has been created by programmers for free use. To be clear, these CMS systems aren't necessarily easy to use and generally require someone with experience to implement. The biggest advantage is that you can customize the site layout (also known as a *template*) to suit your logo, colors, and overall user layout.

The three main free CMS systems to build Websites are Joomla, Drupal, and WordPress. I've used all of them, but my favorite by far is Wordpress. It's easier to modify and set up than the others. More importantly, there are more WordPress professionals available to help build your Website.

Elements of Your Website

Design

What makes good design is relative. Design not only encompasses the visual elements of the Website but also the natural "flow" visitors experience when they visit your site. Certain people may find one Website appealing, while others will hate the way it looks and "feels." Design typically includes the theme, font(s), logo, colors, and layout, all of which contribute to the overall aesthetic and message. Here are few things you should consider when working on your Website design:

- **Theme:** The theme or template you choose for your Website should be consistent throughout all your pages. It should reflect the style and image you want to project on the Web. Good themes are focused, understandable and clean.

- **Font(s):** The font(s) you use should be easy to read, not only for you but also for your intended target audience. For example, if your Website is geared toward the older generation, try to select fonts that are larger and easier to read. I can't count how many Websites I've visited that have horrible, unreadable fonts or poor (ugly, too light, too dark) font colors.

There is a science behind the best fonts to use in a Website. I am fascinated by the psychology of behavioral economics and the experts in this field, such as Derek Halpern. Halpern discussed the psychology of fonts in one of his articles, based on research by Hyunjin Song and Norbert Schwarz. Roger Dooley, the founder of Dooley Direct, LLC, a marketing agency, summarizes the findings of the research as follows:

Research by Hyunjin Song and Norbert Schwarz shows that the way we perceive information can be affected dramatically by how simple or complex the font is. In particular, their work found that a simple font was more likely to get the readers to make a commitment.

The researchers expected that getting people to commit to an exercise regimen would depend on how long they thought the workout would take. A longer estimated time would be a bigger commitment, and people would be less likely to sign up. That's all simple logic, but Song and Schwarz decided to test two groups of subjects. The first group saw the exercises described in a simple font (Arial), while the second group saw the exact same text presented in a harder to read font (Brush).

The results were astounding—the subjects who read the same instructions in the hard to read font estimated that the regimen would take nearly *twice as long,* 15.1 minutes versus 8.2 minutes. Needless to say, the group that thought the exercise would take only 8 minutes was significantly more likely to commit to the regimen.

This basically means that complicated fonts can give people the perception that the task you're asking them to do is difficult: "hard to read" equals "hard to do." Song and Schwarz also discovered that complicated or fancy fonts can give the reader the impression that your product is more valuable. Clearly it's a fine line to walk, because if it's too hard to read, your customers may be turned off. In my opinion, simplicity in the fonts you choose is necessary to walk your customers and visitors through your Website and get them to buy!

- **Logo:** Your logo is usually the first thing visitors notice on your Website, so it's important to create one that portrays what you stand for, is easy to remember, and can be easily *ported* (meaning it can be used both on the Web and in print mediums).

- **Colors:** The colors you use on your Website make a huge impact on how it is perceived. According to KISSmetrics, 93 percent of a consumer's decision-making process comes from visual appearance, and 85 percent comes from color alone. Colors can evoke an emotional response, so when selecting colors for your Website, try to think about the goal of your Website and whom you wish to target.

Content

Content can be made up of text, images, and even videos. Regardless of the purpose of your Website, you want the content therein to be relevant. Relevant content means you are giving visitors a reason to stay and continue to browse. One way to achieve this is by answering a simple question for your visitors: "What's in it for me?" Once you know the right information to place on your Website, consider the following elements of your content:

- **Text:** There are a lot of different things one must consider when making a Website. Many of these are specific to the site's purpose, but a number of general practices can go a long way towards making your page more accessible and easy to comprehend for your visitors. One of these items is the format in which your text shows up.

- **Images:** Imagery helps visitors make an emotional connection to the information you are presenting. Images can help you to display your personality, provide depth for your products, and much, much more.

Navigation

While content is king, it's futile if your visitors can't reach the right information quickly and easily. Your Website navigation needs to be simple, and all the information, easy to find. It shouldn't be difficult for visitors to find their way around your site and get what they need!

Free and Premium Website Solutions

There are several companies that allow you to build free Websites with the option to upgrade to a premium option. Some of the popular ones are Weebly, Wix, Intuit, GoDaddy, Webs, and Network Solutions. My two favorites are Weebly and Wix.

Wix

Three entrepreneurs founded Wix.com in 2006. Based out of Tel Aviv, Israel, this Website works on the concept of "drag and drop" to create a state-of-the-art Website that conforms to the HTML5 code and the various mobile operating systems available. Wix.com is completely free for all users. The Website receives its funding through investors; as a result, this is an ideal Website for startups, small enterprises, and freelancers looking for a platform to launch their online presence. What makes Wix so popular is that you can click anywhere on the page and change the text or access the settings needed to change the content. Wix.com also offers support in a variety of languages: English, Dutch, Spanish, French, Italian, Polish, Portuguese, Russian, and Chinese.

Creating a Website with Wix

Let's start by creating a basic Website:

1. The first step is to login to *www.wix.com*. You will see a landing page.

2. The next step is to click on the **Start Now** option. This will show the pop-up window. Click on the option **Create New Account**.

3. This will bring you to the sign up page. Enter your e-mail address and a password. Click on **Go**.

4. Select the category your business or service falls under and then click **Go**.

5. This will then show you a number of templates. There are two types of templates—free and e-commerce (paid) versions.

6. Wix.com allows you to select **New** templates, **Most Popular** templates or **Blank** templates. (The third option is for people who want to design their own.)

7. Click on **Edit** to edit the template and begin creating your Website. By clicking on **Edit**, you will be directed to the Wix HTML Editor. The first pop-up you see will be the help center. You can review the functions in the video attached or click on **X** to close the video.

How to edit the template

The main reason behind Wix.com's popularity is the ease with which you can edit a template. Let's edit your template and customize it as per your requirements. First, take a look at the tools on the top left hand-side of the page. It has the following options:

PAGE: This option is used to add/delete and reorder pages on your Website. All you have to do is click on the predefined name in the template and make the changes. Click on the blue icon next to the name. This will show another pop-up window. All you have to do is fill in the fields. You can use this setting to enter your SEO settings for the page. The Wix editor also allows you to duplicate pages and the settings as well as delete pages. Click on the relevant option on the top of the page to accomplish this.

If you want to add a brand-new page without duplication, go back to the main Pages option and click on **Add Page**. You will have to name the page and fill in all the fields.

DESIGN: The Wix editor gives you a lot of different design functions. When you click on the design option, you will get the following three options: Background, Colors, and Fonts. When you click on any one of the options, you will see a number of different options available. All you have to do is click on the choice that suits you and the template will be updated automatically. This option allows you to see in real time how the Website will look. Neat!

ADD: The Wix Editor also allows you to add additional elements to the Web page. All you have to do is click on any one item; then select the style and the placement on the page. However, do not add items just for the sake of adding. An item should be added only if it plays an important role on the Website.

SETTINGS: Wix editor gives you total control over your Website's settings. There are six basic settings and two premium or paid settings. The six basic settings are as below.

1. **Site Address:** This will be your user name.wix.com/site_name

2. **SEO:** This stands for your search engine optimization settings. These settings will dictate how your website is ranked in all the search engines. Use proper descriptions and keywords to enhance the visibility of the site.

3. **Mobile View:** These settings are related to how your Website will look on various mobile browsers. Remember that the Website and all details related to the owner should be clearly visible on any mobile operating system.

4. **Contact Information:** This allows you to add all your information to be displayed on the Web and mobile operating systems.

5. **Social Media Profile:** Your social media profile is an important part of your website. Hence, the Wix editor enables you to add your information across various social media platforms.

6. **Social Settings:** This setting is exclusively for Facebook. You can upload a thumbnail of your website to display on Facebook. You can also add plugins for Facebook (for example, a "Like" button) to your Website. This allows you to have a more integrated Facebook experience.

7. **Statistics:** This is a premium service offered by Wix. Under this service, users can track their Website's performance and analyze statistics such as traffic.

8. **Favicon:** Another premium service offered by Wix. This one allows you to upload a 16-by-16 pixel icon that will show up whenever your Website is viewed.

APP MARKET: The app market is an applications marketplace that offers a number of free and paid applications from Wix.com and from other service providers. All you have to do is select the application and place it on your Website.

Wix's premium services

Other than the free basic service, Wix.com offers a number of yearly and monthly premium plans. These plans are divided into four categories— E-commerce, Unlimited, Combo, and Connect Domain plans.

1. **E-commerce:** This option is best for small and medium enter- prises. The package costs $16.17 per month if you select the annual billing plan, and 19.90 USD per month if you select the monthly billing plan. Wix.com offers 20 GB of storage and 10 GB of bandwidth under this plan.

2. **Unlimited:** This option is best for entrepreneurs and free- lancers. The package costs $12.42 per month if you select the annual billing plan and 15.95 USD per month if you select the monthly billing plan. Wix.com offers 10 GB of storage and unlimited bandwidth under this plan.

3. **Combo:** The option is best for personal use. The package costs $8.25 per month if you select the annual billing plan and 10.95 USD per month if you select the monthly billing plan. Wix.com offers 3 GB of storage and 2 GB of bandwidth under this plan.

4. **Connect Domain:** This is the most basic option available. The package costs $4.08 per month if you select the annual billing plan and 5.95 USD per month if you select the monthly billing plan. Wix.com offers 500 MB of storage and 1 GB of band- width under this plan.

The features covered under the first three plans are:

- Option of adding a favicon
- Option of mobile ads
- Option of connecting your domain
- Free hosting options
- Google Analytics options

- Premium support options
- No Wix ads

The features covered under the basic plan are:
- Option of connecting your domain
- Free hosting options
- Google Analytics options
- Premium support options

Wix.com offers the following additional services under all premium plans:
- Free hosting
- No fees for setup
- Wide range of templates
- Fully customizable pages

As you can see, the popularity of this Website stems from its large number of tools and customization options offered under the basic package. The multilingual support ensures that anyone from across the globe can use the basic as well as premium services. Wix also offers affordable and well-equipped premium services, as well as a well-designed support page that answers all your questions. You can even contact the staff via their forum or their toll-free number. For all these reasons and more, this Website remains one of the best options for setting up your presence on the World Wide Web.

Weebly

David Rusenko, Chris Fanini, and Dan Veltri cofounded Weebly in 2006 when they were 22-year-old students at Penn State University. The founders wanted to provide an easier way to build professional Websites without having to know coding. Their collaboration and funding from investors saw the site develop into a major player in the "drag and drop" Website creation sector. The initial versions of the Website did not have CSS and HTML editing, but in spite of these infelicities, the Website managed to register a million users. The Website added the CSS and HTML editing functions in 2009. As of this writing, some estimate that Weebly.com has close to 12 million users.

Creating a Website with Weebly

Let us take a step-by-step look at how you can create a basic Webpage on Weebly:

1. Log in to *www.weebly.com*.

2. You have two options for joining. You can login via your Facebook login ID and password, or you can enter your name and e-mail and select a password. Click on **Sign Up**—it's free!

3. Weebly will direct you to the themes page. You can move your mouse over the theme you want and click on **Choose**.

4. Select the font color and then click on **Choose**. This will direct you to the Website editor of Weebly.com

5. There are three options for your Website address: the first option is a sub-domain within Weebly.com; the second option is to register for a unique Website in your name; and the third option is to directly connect to your own Website. While the first and the last are the basic options, the second option falls under the premium services.

6. Once you select the option, click on **Continue**.

7. You'll see two options: **Plan My Site** or **Build My Site**. The best way to create a useful and attractive Website is to plan it first.

8. When you click on **Plan My Site**, you are presented with the following page.

9. Scroll down on the Welcome page and click on **Next Step**. This will take you to the Site Goals option.

10. On this page, you will have to enter the reason for setting up the site, the goals of your site, and the information you want to include on your site.

11. Once you have updated this information, you can scroll down and click on **Next Step**. If you don't wish to add any more information, click on **Mark This Step Complete**.

12. When you click on **Next Step**, you'll be asked to look at some other sites to get ideas. Click on **Next Step** to move ahead.

13. This will bring you to the Page Layouts information page. On the page, click on the link **Page Layout Options** to start building your page. The Website editor is divided into **Basic**, **Structure**, **Media**, **Commerce**, and **More Options**.

The options under **Basic** are as follows:

▶ **Title**—This allows you to add a text title or a logo as your title of your Web page.

▶ **Text**—This allows you to add details to your Web page.

▶ **Image+ Text**—This allows you to add pictures and a brief description.

▶ **Image**—This allows you to add pictures.

▶ **Gallery**—This allows you to create an image gallery.

▶ **Slideshow**—This allows you to create a slideshow.

▶ **Map**—This allows you to add maps for directions to your business.

▶ **Contact form**—This allows you to add your contact details.

The options under **Structure** are as follows:

▶ **Divider**—This allows you to divide your page into different sections.

▶ **Columns**—This allows you to add columns.

▶ **Search Box**—This is an option offered under premium services.

▶ **Button**—This allows you to add buttons to your page.

The options under **Media** are as follows:

▶ **HD Video**—This premium service allows you to divide upload a high-definition video to your page.

▶ **Audio**—This premium service allows you to add an audio clip to your page.

▶ **Document**—This allows you to add any document.

▶ **YouTube**—This allows you to add a YouTube video.

▶ **. Doc file**—This allows you to add a Word document.

The options under **Commerce** are as follows.

▶ **Product**—This allows you to setup a Google or PayPal online store.

▶ **Google AdSense**—This allows you to link your Ad words account to your Website.

The options under **More Settings** are as follows.

▶ **Block Quote**—This allows you to add a quotation for any product you want to sell.

▶ **Embed Code**—This option allows you to customize the HTML settings for your site.

▶ **Poll**—This allows you to setup a poll with *www. polldaddy.com*.

▶ **Social Icons**—This allows adding details about your social media accounts.

▶ **RSVP form**—This allows your readers to confirm their participation in any event organized by you.

▶ **Survey**—This allows you to offer the option of a survey to your readers.

▶ **Feed Reader**—This allows you to add an RSS newsreader to your Website.

▶ **Bookings**—This allows you to set up a calendar and schedule on your Website

▶ **Forums**—This allows you to set up a forum on your Website.

14. In order to add more pages and edit the name of any page, click on the **Pages** header at the top of the page. Similarly, click on the **Design** header to change the design elements of the page. Once you have completed designing your Web page, click on the **Publish** option on the top right-hand side of the page.

Congratulations, your Website is up and running!

Premium options

Weebly.com offers you the option of two premium accounts: the Starter account and the Pro account. The cost of the starter account is 3.29 USD per month and the cost of the Pro account is 6.63 USD per month. You get 100 USD of free AdWords advertising in both accounts. You get 100 MB of storage in the starter account and 250 MB of storage in the Pro account.

Common options offered under both premium accounts:

- **Customized Domain Name**—You can create your own domain name.

- **Statistics**—The Website gives you access to a detailed traffic and visitor analysis.

- **Custom Footer**—You can add more details to the footer of your page.

- **Remove the Weebly Link**—You can remove the link to *www. weebly.com*.

- **Favicon**—You can add an icon that will show up whenever someone sees your Website.

- **Premium Support**—The Website offers you a high level of customer support.

The following options are only available with a Pro account:

- **Site Search**—You can add a search engine option to the Website.

- **Header Slideshow**—Allows you to add interactive content to your Website.

- **HD video and audio**—Allows you to add high-definition videos and audio clips to your Website.

- **Password protection**—Allows you to restrict access to certain pages.
- **Editor**—Allows you to define who can edit your pages.

Support options

Weebly also offers you a detailed support page. This support page gives you a detailed walk-through of the entire process. It also has a video that trains you by showing you how to use the Website. In case you still need help, all you have to do is scroll down the support page and click on **Ask Us a Question**. You can prioritize your request or just make it a normal request. This helps the Website tailor its response time.

Like others in this sector, Weebly offers freelancers and small entrepreneurs the perfect way to set up and expand their online presence. What sets this Website apart is the huge number of features, the extremely simplistic interface, and the very short time it takes to learn how to create Web pages. Its huge popularity indicates that this is one Website creator that should not be missed. If you are looking to create your Website for free and do not want run-of-the-mill options, visit *www.weebly.com* for a professional Website experience.

Chapter 18

Raising Money

You have a great idea and now all you need is the money to fund it. Friends, family, and fools are usually the first stop on the funding train. However, I strongly discourage people from seeking funding for their start-up from friends or family. They are generally the worst people to have as investors.

Friends and family usually aren't sophisticated investors and don't have the disposable funds to invest in your untested start-up. For every success story of parents draining their retirement savings to fund their son's new social networking site for cats, there are untold numbers of failures. This can make Thanksgiving and Christmas a lot more awkward. People who aren't used to investing in early-stage companies aren't good for your sanity because you'll be spending a lot of time calming them down.

I previously shared the story of Craig, whose mother was willing to mortgage the house and take a loan to help fund his idea for a fried chicken franchise. Entrepreneurs who take money from friends and family fail for the following four reasons:

1. Expectations aren't adequately managed. Entrepreneurs fail to update their investors about the progress of the business. In addition, there's a failure to update the time line of funds being used.

2. They borrow money that friends and family can't afford to lose. In other words, it's not discretionary and therefore there's more pressure to make the start-up work. Unfortunately, there are a lot of things that are out of the control of the founders.

3. The agreement lacks professionalism in that there isn't a formal agreement or contract that is notarized and which outlines the responsibility of the entrepreneur.

4. There's a very large chance the business will fail. The business, investment money, and relationship will all be gone.

I can hear you now: "It takes money to make money!" That's sort of true, but more often it's an excuse many use to chase money they don't need to buy things they don't need. I'm a large advocate of getting your first customer and then your second customer. This is an important element of bootstrapping. *Bootstrapping* is a term to describe an entrepreneur using very little money to start his or her company. It's derived from the phrase "pulling yourself up by the bootstraps." The term also describes a start-up's ability to be self-sustaining, without outside investment.

You don't need large amounts of money to get your business off the ground unless you're building something completely from scratch. In the 1990s, money from angel investors and venture capitalists were thrown at everything that was a dot-com. If you were starting a Web-based company, you needed to hire Web designers, buy Web servers, and create the infrastructure. You don't need any of that anymore. Websites can be built for less than $250 and free open-source software is readily available.

So if you can easily build a Website for less money, why would you need to raise money? You shouldn't consider starting a business if you don't have at least $1,000 to start. We are taught by society to write a business plan and use it to raise money. The majority of business plans are comprised of assumptions, so how does using a business plan make any sense? Your business has to prove or validate that the concept works. In other words, you have to show there's a market whose problem your idea solves. This is the importance of getting your first customer. Customers who buy your product or service provide your business with the cash flow to fund and support future operations.

Targeting a specific niche increases the likelihood of getting your first customer because you can adequately solve a problem that niche has. You're not all things to all people and you can easily identify what potential customers want by being specific. The majority of you have a skill or product that you believe solves a problem for a niche. Provide your solution to that group and you will have your first customer.

Neil Patel is a digital marketing entrepreneur who helps businesses and individuals with their marketing by providing useful analytics. He is the cofounder of Crazy Egg, a company that helps individuals and businesses determine what visitors are doing when they visit their site. Neil is also the cofounder of KISSmetrics, which provides a service that shows who visited, their actions, and how companies can use that information to improve sales and customer experience by tracking the lifelong value of the customer. Neil writes a marketing blog for individuals and small businesses called Quick Sprout, and highlighted the importance of specifically targeting a niche. (Visit his blogging Website, Quicksprout.com, and subscribe for e-mail updates of new content.)

Think about the products you use and the ones you love. What's different about your behavior with the products you love? What is it about the product or company that puts you over the top? Here are some ways businesses go about creating passionate behavior:

► Donate money to charity or adopt a social cause—Toms Shoes does this by donating a pair of shoes for every one that is bought.

► Provide extraordinary customer service—Zappos and Nordstrom are two companies known for providing excellent customer service. For example, Nordstrom has a lifetime return policy.

► Create usable products—people love Basecamp not because it has the most features, but because it's really easy to use.

► Appeal to beliefs—American Apparel only sells clothing that is made in America, as some people feel that wearing clothing made in other countries is hurting the American economy.

► Go above and beyond the call of duty—make sure the customer's experience exceeds expectations.

Creating passion doesn't have to be a direct relation of your product or service. You can also provide passion through your interactions with customers and by connecting with the niche community. For example, Karla from Bellybuttonboutique.com sells clothing and products for pregnant women. She continues to interact with her customers via forums and social media. She conceived the idea for an online retailer after dealing with a challenging pregnancy. Her customers can relate to her and appreciate the content she shares online with customers. People love her content so much because she educates her ideal customer so they can make more informed purchases.

When trying to acquire customers, focusing on a specific market does the following:

- It's cheaper to make changes to your product or service because you have a small segment to focus on.

- It's a lot more manageable to deal with feedback from customers.

- It's cheaper to manufacture your product because it's a limited quantity. This also serves a purpose of validating your idea.

Bank Loans Are a Waste of Time

To review: the two reasons business plans are bullshit are: 1) no one will read them; and 2) they are works of fiction. The person writing your business plan for you will not even read it. The misconception is you need a business plan to present to investors and the bank. The reality is that they, too, know that your business plan is bullshit. You may well ask, "How could they know, Ebong? They have never seen my business or the plan!" There is actually no need for the bank and investors to see it.

Banks and investors do not need to see a business plan because they don't believe anything that's in the plan. I have business relationships with several commercial bankers in addition to clients who have loans with some of these banks. Banks primarily lend money on the basis of your past performance in business. Having good credit is a must, but it is not the linchpin to a successful answer. You have no past performance if you have just started out on your own. Your idea, market, and business are unproven and, according to most statistics, destined for failure. As of this writing, banks are just not lending money, which is part of the problem with the anemic economic recovery in 2011 and 2012. In my experience, banks prefer to lend to companies and people who do not need the money. If you are fortunate enough to have a line of credit or loan from the bank, the bank may cancel your existing line of credit for no apparent reason.

When I started my clothing line in 2008, I had a $25,000 line of credit from one of the nation's biggest banks. During the economic crisis, the bank unceremoniously canceled my line of credit with a simple form letter and no explanation—even though there were no delinquencies and my payments were current. It was one of the catalysts that ultimately led to me closing the business.

Former *Huffington Post* economics reporter Bonnie Kavoussi chronicled the massive problem small businesses face trying to acquire loans from banks, in a *Huffington Post* article titled "Small Businesses Struggling To Get Loans: Federal Reserve Study." According to a Kavoussi, it has gotten harder for small businesses to get loans. The number of U.S. small business loans, defined as $1 million or less, declined 5 percent last year, according to a recent study by the Small Business Administration. The dollar amount of small business loans declined 7 percent.

I will sum it up for you: Banks ain't lending to you for your idea, start-up, or invention! This is why the idea of wasting your time and money on a business plan leads you astray. If no one will read it and no one will lend to you—why write it? You have to start your business idea on your own. These are the best times to start a business with next to nothing. You no longer need $100,000 for computer equipment, servers, and Web developers. Good Websites are cheap to build. E-mail is almost free (if you want to personalize your e-mail). There are tremendous amounts of free and creative marketing ideas to build your customers and audience.

Venture Capital and Angel Investors (Another Waste of Time)

Fabrice Grinda's experiences have followed the typical American Dream rollercoaster story. Immigrant comes to America, learns skills, learns the market, starts a business, teeters on the brink of financial ruin, and then rises from the rubble, phoenix-like and victorious. Lather, rinse, and repeat (as if the last painful start-up experience was not enough abuse). Fabrice is an angel investor, avid blogger, and experienced serial entrepreneur who has founded, built, and sold several businesses.

After graduating summa cum laude from Princeton University in 1996, Fabrice joined McKinsey & Co. Corporate life was not for him and soon left to start and serve as the CEO of Aucland, SA, which was one of the top three auction Websites in 1998. In 2001, he started Zingy, Inc., which he built into one of the largest wireless media companies in the Americas while successfully closing deals with some of the top wireless providers in the world.

I started following Fabrice's career after listening to a podcast interview on Greg Galant's Venture Voice. He had just sold the mobile phone multimedia ringtone, games, and wallpaper company Zingy, Inc. for approximately $80 million in 2004. Fabrice's story of highs and lows were extremely engaging, as was his use of anecdotal imagery. I was most interested in his ability to raise money for start-ups in industries that were new at the time. More importantly, I sense the parallel between his experiences and my own. Many of you will read this and say, "Well, it's easy to start a business when you have money and don't need loans." True, but the reality is it is not about loans or the old adage of how "it takes money to make money." Fabrice started the same way many of us did.

When I interviewed him in 2013, he had recently left his most recent company, OLX, Inc., which he started with his business partner, Alec Oxenford, in 2006. They sought to build the largest free local classified site in the world. Fabrice served as co-CEO and drove the company's business development, investor relations, M&A, and product development efforts. OLX now has more than 300 employees and is present in more than 90 countries and 50 languages with more than 150 million unique visitors per month.

Scaling or growing a company is both a science and an art form but without money it is merely a trite saying. Taking a company like Zingy from $0 to $200 million in revenue is never luck. Due to the internet bubble bursting in 2001, it was nearly impossible to raise capital for anything. Fabrice used his own money to start Zingy but more importantly, he did not take a salary for years and struggled to make payroll several times. The science is stretching dollars and pennies and the art form is convincing employees to stick around while you figure out ways to pay them. Our conversation or interview via Skype (more conversation) lasted more than an hour while Fabrice was on a month-long vacation in the Dominican Republic!

As you read this in your home office, on the subway or in a park, remember that at some point in the beginning we wondered how to get money to grow the business. It is important to remember that most of you will not need venture capital or angel investors. Fabrice is mainly coming from that perspective. These are a few of the suggestions from Fabrice (my thoughts are in boldface, in parentheses):

► Beg friends and family for money **(only as a last resort!)**.

► Don't pay yourself **(you really don't have a choice at the beginning)**.

► Beg your developer friends to build the software for you **(important!)**.

► Give sweat equity to whomever you need in the early stages of the company.

► Penny pinch on everything **(except the quality of your product or services)**.

Get your first customer; then, get even more customers to fund the growth of your company. In the next chapter, we'll explore the lynchpin for doing just that—sales.

Chapter 19
The Four S's: Sales

Selling is a science. That is not just a catchy phrase, but a reality. It is not about schmoozing customers or playing golf with prospects. Successful entrepreneurs understand the science of sales and use it to build their business. Scientists have spent years studying the concept of behavioral economics. Behavioral economics or behavioral finance is the study of the effects of social and emotional factors on the economic decisions made by individuals and institutions and the consequences for market prices. There are three prevalent themes in behavioral economics:

1. **Heuristics:** People often make decisions based on rules of thumb and not strict logic (short-cuts).

2. **Framing:** People tend to rely on collection of anecdotes, experiences, and stereotypes when trying to understand situations and respond to events (stories).

3. **Market inefficiencies:** In some cases, irrational decisions and unexplainable behaviors in the market play a role (in other words, we can't always explain people's decisions).

Selling your product and services is the single most important thing you do as a business owner. You cannot make money without sales. You cannot hire employees and scale your company without sales. Sure, you can raise equity capital or borrow money, but the underlying assumption is that your company will make sales and money in the future. Sales are the single biggest factor of corporate sustainability and one of the biggest reasons businesses fail.

Throughout my career, I have been enamored with the concept of sales and spent time and money to learn more about it. I noticed that small number of salespeople and business development professionals were closing big deals. In addition, they were selling with ease and without having to work that hard (in appearance, at least). The concept of pattern recognition presented itself to me once again. These salespeople appeared to be able to influence prospects to buy. When I spoke and met with business and marketing gurus such as Gary Vaynerchuk, Yanik Silver, Ramit Sethi, and Fabrice Grinda, all of them said they swear by a seminal book on the psychology of sales and influence, written by Dr. Robert Cialdini.

Dr. Robert Cialdini has spent his entire career researching the science of influence earning him an international reputation as an expert in the fields of persuasion, compliance, and negotiation. He is best known for his 1984 book on persuasion and marketing, *Influence: The Psychology of Persuasion*. *Influence* has sold more than two million copies and has been translated into 26 languages. It has been listed on the *New York Times* business best-seller list. Basically, you need to buy this book and read it!

Dr. Cialdini shares what he calls the Six Principles of Influence (also known as the Six Weapons of Influence), which increase the likelihood of successful persuasion. These principles/weapons are:

1. Reciprocation
2. Commitment and Consistency
3. Social Proof
4. Liking
5. Scarcity
6. Authority

Reciprocation

Generally speaking, people are likely to return or reciprocate a favor. People experience a deep obligation to make a concession or repay someone who has done the same for us. If a friend pays for your lunch at work, you are more likely to return the favor by paying for their lunch at a later date. This is mainly the reason companies offer free product samples, services, and content marketing.

In Victor Hugo's 19-century classic novel, *Les Misérables*, petty criminal Jean Valjean steals the Bishop's silverware and silver plates and runs off. He is arrested and brought back to the Bishop. However, the Bishop admonishes Valjean (in front of the police) for forgetting to also take the silver candlesticks that he had given Valjean, reminding Valjean of his "promise" to use the silver to become an honest man. Valjean then feels compelled to turn his life around.

Commitment and Consistency

People are more likely to honor an oral or written commitment because they feel that reneging on that commitment says something about their self-image. For example, a woman working on her laptop at Starbucks tells a neighbor she needs to step out and asks him to keep his eye on her laptop while she is gone. If the neighbor commits to watching the laptop, he will likely be much more vocal if someone approaches it.

Social Proof

People will follow the actions of others. In short, monkey see, monkey do. This is why you see a lot of testimonials in advertisements for products and services. Showing growing numbers of users or customers increases the likelihood that others will follow suit because it eases the minds of worrying customers. Similarly, most people will search online for product reviews before purchasing a product. EBay uses this principle via seller ratings. Buyers feel more comfortable with sellers that have more and higher ratings.

Liking

Few people would be surprised to learn that, as a rule, we most prefer to say yes to the requests of someone we know and like. I have also heard this principle as "People tend to do business with people they like." This simple rule is used in hundreds of ways by total strangers to get us to comply with their requests. Dr. Cialdini cites the growth of multilevel marketing companies like Tupperware. Salespeople host home Tupperware parties with people they either already know or have a slight connection to. Studies show that people like to do business with people:

a. who are attractive, dress, and present well;

b. who are physically similar to them;

    c.   who offer compliments and attempt to connect with others;

    d.   whom they can relate to because of cultural similarities or experiences.

Authority

People tend to follow and obey instructions from a recognized authority because this provides us with a valuable shortcut for deciding how to act in a crisis situation. When a doctor tells a patient a diagnosis, the patient is more inclined to listen to the doctor than to research on his or her own (absent the Internet). Conforming to authority figures is a practice that has been taught to us from an early age. For example, parents and teachers knew more than we did, and we found that taking their advice proved beneficial—partly because of their greater wisdom, and partly because they controlled our lives. Each of the following three types of symbols of authority is worth a separate look:

1. **Titles:** People with titles establish authority to their audience. Examples are doctors, lawyers, and CPAs. Other professionals with designations, experiences, and awards serve this purpose, as well. This also explains why you often see doctors or dentists in lab coats featured in commercials about medicines.

2. **Clothing:** A second kind of authority symbol that can trigger outward compliance is clothing. Though more tangible than a title, the cloak of authority can also be faked. Examples police officers, military personnel, and con men in expensive suits.

3. **Trappings:** This principle represents expensive things like jewelry, cars, "toys"—stuff that denotes status and accomplishment. Dr. Cialdini discusses that studies show people tend to respect more and give more leeway to those with trappings when they are being sold to. A common example would be the salesperson at the car dealership who drives an expensive car. There is a tendency to believe that people like this are successful and therefore more trustworthy.

Scarcity

The less available a product is, the more demand there will be for it. This explains why infomercials use the "only for a limited time" technique. The idea of an inability to purchase a product because it is limited is a psychological trigger that gets customers to act quicker than they otherwise would have.

Contrast

Cialdini also discusses another principle of human perception, called contrast, which I feel is equally important for small-business owners because it's so easy to implement. Research studies show that people will compare and contrast when faced with deciding between two or more items. This is why a sales associate independently upsells add-ons to you when you buy a product. For example, if you're buying a $25,000 car, the salesperson will independently offer add-ons or options such as a GPS system (at $1,000) and a 6-disc CD changer (for $500). The $1,500 for the options is negligible compared to $25,000 for the car, so it's easy for him or her to sell these options to you.

Expensive = Good

Another aspect of contrast is the idea that expensive equals good. We are generally taught that the higher the cost/price of an item or service, the better the quality. For example, in fashion, a Louis Vuitton handbag may retail for $1,000, while another handbag from Macy's will retail for $100. The initial belief is that the more expensive bag is of much higher quality. Another example Dr. Cialdini uses is a shop owner whose assistant mistakenly doubles the price of jewelry that she was previously unable to sell. The increase in price leads to the shop quickly selling out of the jewelry.

Do you ever wonder why a salesperson uses the techniques he or she does? Some of you may think that all sales is manipulation, but a lot of life is. People will buy your product or services if they need them, not because you manipulate or coerce them into doing so. They buy your products and services because you solve a problem they have. It is your responsibility to understand the psychological component in sales and use these principles of persuasion and perception judiciously. The principle of persuasion makes it a little easier for you to share your message and skills with potential customers. If you do not focus on the system and process of selling, you will not be in business very long.

Another important sales principle I learned from behavioral science expert Derek Halpern is called "arguing against one's own interest." An example would be telling a customer that your product or service is not for everyone. It may appear counterintuitive for a salesperson to tell a customer that "not everyone will use my product/service, and it may not be for you," but it's a pretty common technique nonetheless.

People tend to do what is in their best interest. As a result, that belief is a shortcut we take when evaluating information we receive from a salesperson. So when a salesperson tells a customer something that is contrary to their best interest, they tend to believe them. I have a friend of mine who is a lawyer in private practice. He told me that he often tells prospective clients who try to haggle with him that there are other lawyers out there that may be a better fit. He goes as far as to present them with the contact list of these lawyers. Many of these prospective clients stop haggling and choose him for representation—likely because they feel that he would rather give up a client than take one that is not a good fit. Remember the saying, "I have nothing to gain by telling you this"? That's a perfect example of this technique.

■■■

Now that you have a better understanding of sales and the methods of persuasion, in the next chapter we'll discuss how to use some of those techniques to help land your first customer.

Chapter 20

Getting Your First Customer

So how do you make money from your idea and business? Land your first customer and then multiply the process by 10—it's that easy! No, it's not easy, nor will it happen quickly, but following the steps I outline in this chapter will help accelerate the process.

First, you must address the problem you're solving and the result (benefit) your customers receive. Remember, there is only one reason why people spend money—to solve a problem. Now that you know that, it should be easy to get customers and sales, right? Well, no, because entrepreneurs tend not to focus on solving their customers' problems; instead, they focus on their idea and fall in love with it. The truth is, customers don't care about your business, product, and service unless and until you can tell them what's in it for them.

For example, let's say you are a public relations specialist and you feel that your experiences will make customers want to hire you. You have excellent relationships in the media; you're well-known, you love your work, and you care about it. Know this: *Your customer does not care about you or your accolades.* Your customers only care about what's in it for them. How do you solve their problem? They won't hire you because you're an expert PR person; they will hire you because your relationships increase their chances of getting media attention and exposure for *their* business (also known as "the problem"). The customer appearing on the evening news as an expert will give her company more credibility and could lead to more sales.

If you present yourself as "Expert Public Relations Representative—Check Out My Website!" nobody is going to listen. You quickly become a commodity wherein potential customers cannot distinguish between service providers. If you say, "Get the recognition and professionalism your company deserves by appearing on a major network TV—click here," then you will pique your customer's interest in your services.

Before the great Steve Jobs introduced the iPod we used Sony cassette and CD players. Tapes and compact discs had limited storage space; you could only have one album per CD or tape. People didn't know they had a storage problem until the iPod came along. How did Jobs get people to embrace the iPod? He leveraged salient or important points that addressed the problems customers already had, but didn't necessarily know they had! The iPod ranges from 2 gigabytes to 160 gigabytes of memory. Saying how many songs the iPod holds instead of telling customers how much memory it has, addresses the important problem. I care about how many songs my iPod holds because that's how I judge storage—by number of songs. You have to do the same for your business.

Being specific with your niche market allows you to focus on what its problems are and how you can provide the solution or solutions. In other words, it's about the problems of your customers, not what advantages your product or service offers. When presenting a product or service to your customers, point out the problem they're having, share how you will solve their problem, and communicate that message using salient or important points.

I was recently speaking with a friend who runs the IT department of a large corporation. Alex is responsible for implementing IT policy, IT systems, and security. Occasionally, Alex finds opportunities to save the company money and time by implementing new software and systems. In a recent example, Alex found that automating a purchasing process would make it faster for products to be manufactured. Automating the new process would cost approximately $10,000. When Alex pitched the idea to management, management said no because they didn't feel the need to spend the money to improve a process that they felt didn't enhance their bottom line.

Although a lot of these opportunities offer large cost savings, Alex often has difficulty getting management to make the initial upfront investment. Sometimes management doesn't understand the bigger picture; they've managed to carve out a small niche in the organization, so there's no incentive for them to think outside the realm of their own environment unless Alex can successfully answer this one question: "What's in it for me/ us?"

"What's in it for me?" is the only question you have to answer when you're trying to convince a customer to do business with you. Of course Alex isn't a small-business owner, but the situation is the same. He had a great idea that can save the company money and needs to sell management on it. The problem is, Alex wasn't using salient points to answer the question of what would be in it for them. Going back to the iPod, I don't care how many gigabytes my iPod has, but do I care about how many songs it can hold. Using salient points means understanding what problem your customer wants solved. Alex needs to find out what is driving management; in this case, it's their annual bonus. Management receives a bonus for either higher revenues or cutting costs. Instead of sharing the benefits of improving the process, Alex should show how spending $10,000 now will save $100,000 in expenses over two years. The savings translates into bigger bonuses for management, and voila! Management now knows what's in it for them!

Getting your first paying customer is obviously important for growing your business. It also provides you with money, confidence, idea valida-tion, and opportunities to document a process. Remember that business plans do not account for your first customer, but instead rely on a plethora of assumptions based on other assumptions. Your first customer provides you with important real-life feedback that a business plan can never come close to providing.

Here are some reasons why your first customer is so important:

- **Money and capital:** The central goal of a business is for cus-tomers to fund operations and earn profits.

- **Business confidence:** As we have discussed in previous chap-ters, fears and doubts stop more people from reaching success than failure does. Many people deal with self-doubt and nay-sayers when they start a business. We build a resume of success after each customer, and that gives us the confidence to go after the next five customers.

- **Idea validation:** Your first customer serves as validation that your idea works. Ideas are plentiful but worthless unless someone pays you for them. You increase the chances of validating an idea if you solve a problem that your customers need solved. It's pretty simple!

As you know, I played professional basketball after graduating from college. Before I played my first professional season in Switzerland, I joined an evangelical Christian sports ministry basketball team called Athletes in Action (AIA). The team was comprised of former college basketball players who use basketball as a method to minister to others. Our AIA team went to China, Taiwan, and North Korea to play against their national basketball teams. It was an amazing trip, and having the ability to not only travel but to spend a lot of time in Asia was a blessing. I built tremendously strong relationships that crossed many cultural barriers. Our goal was to play basketball and then share our mission of faith with anyone who would listen. Many of the Taiwanese people listened to my personal story and experiences. What I noticed was it was easier for me to share my faith with absolute strangers than with people I knew. Sharing your new business idea with friends, family, and business connections is imperative for your success. As evidenced in my experiences in Asia, I came to realize that I exert more influence in my immediate environment than I realized, despite my trepidation. More importantly, overcoming the fear and uncomfortable feelings of sharing your new business with your network could be the source of your first client. The point of my Athletes in Action story is to illustrate the importance of sharing your message and business with your milieu, as you generally wield more influence with them then you do with strangers.

Another way to get your first customer is to leverage the relationships you have with your current or former employer. When I started out as a CPA, a lot of my subsequent contracts came from projects I had previously worked on for my prior employer. In another example, RedPoint Consulting is a consulting company that was started by two IT professionals who previously worked for an agency of the Federal government. They had been working for the agency for several years and understood the needs of similar agencies. They decided to go out on their own, and when they formed their company, their first customer was the very agency they had been working with for the last several years.

Tap Into Your Immediate Environment

People generally like to do business with those they know, like, and trust. This explains why your first customers come from those you have spent time with or have worked with in the past. After a certain age, most professionals should have an established network of contacts. Here are a few more suggestions on how to acquire your first client:

- ▶ Reach out to your professional circle via e-mail and ask them to suggest people you could meet with to offer your services.

- ▶ Search on LinkedIn for potential customers who might need your services.

- ▶ Search Facebook for friends who currently work in the same industry. Find their e-mail addresses and e-mail them directly. Don't e-mail them through Facebook.

- ▶ Make a list of people and businesses who would be ideal customers. The list should only include about 10 to 20 people at the most. Find them on Twitter and connect with them.

- ▶ Join the chamber of commerce in your area and attend their various networking events.

- ▶ Join associations that are relevant to your industry and attend their events. Ask the association for a list of companies that fit your particular area of interest. Participate in events that your targets will attend.

Chapter 21

Content Marketing and Storytelling

Traditional advertising and marketing are dead. This is a bold statement, but it is true. You'll realize this if you take a look around the media landscape. Yes, companies are still spending millions of dollars on Super Bowl ads, but even with those ads, you will still see a larger social media presence. Every network places Twitter hash tags in the corner of your television set. Companies, brands, and personalities offer their names and Twitter handles so viewers can follow them.

In his multimillion best-seller, *Crush It*, Gary Vaynerchuk talks about why billboards no longer work: "People aren't looking at billboards; they aren't even looking at the road anymore!" Television has a similar problem, although not to the same extent. People are muting commercials or using DVRs to skip them entirely. An even bigger issue is that there is no real method of knowing who watched your television commercial and whether they were even interested.

There is another problem in the marketing community. Entrepreneurs and small-business owners think using social media platforms such as Pinterest, Twitter, and Facebook are a waste of time because using them rarely leads to customer conversion. In other words, posts don't necessarily lead to sales. As an example, Twitter made interacting with people a lot easier, but it still has to be proper and authentic interaction. Too many small business owners take short cuts to social media interaction and then wonder why it doesn't work. Twitter, Facebook, Pinterest, and all the rest are not extensions of billboards and television. Using them effectively requires hard and consistent work, finding relevant content that your audience actually gives a crap about. The bigger brands fail to understand that, because you will often see posts about a particular item they sell. It is basically a billboard. Do not blast out constant announcements. Share information that is relevant to your audience and is both engaging and enriching. This is the way marketing via social media works best.

Why is this important? Because too many entrepreneurs throw around ideas of marketing and advertising. They hire a marketing company, create ads, and throw money around just to get customers. I would rather speak to three highly qualified prospective clients than have my message sent to 100 potential clients whom I know little about. Marketing is something of a science, just as selling is. No one wants to be sold. Moreover, most people hate selling! So how do you bridge the gap between two worlds that are clearly very far apart?

The goal is to show people what they need and then give them exactly that. It is not about selling stuff but educating them. It is never about you or what can you do for a customer. The better question is "What are your problems and how can I fix them?" Personally, I have sold more products and services to people after educating them on my area of focus. Have you ever noticed a salesperson in a store educating a customer on what to wear with her new shoes? Many entrepreneurs feel as though they are being taken advantage of when they educate a customer. This is also known as a "brain drain," when potential customers take your hard-earned knowledge and information for free, with no reason to pay you for it afterward. In my experience this is rarely the norm. Remember Robert Cialdini and his book *Influence*? One of the principles is reciprocation—give to get. Give your current and prospective customers useful and business-focused content that they can use to improve their own lives. This doesn't mean that you should give them "fluff" and then wonder why no one is interested in your company. You have to provide usable and valuable content to people that actually betters their lives!

Content Marketing

Copyblogger.com is a content marketing Website founded by Brian Clark in 2006. In addition to being the pioneer of content marketing, Brian is also a former attorney, real estate broker, and serial entrepreneur. Brian built three successful offline businesses using online marketing techniques before moving to a completely online business model. The result of that move was Copyblogger Media—an innovative company that provides the advice and solutions that empowers people to successfully grow their businesses through social media and online marketing. (As a side note, you should subscribe to and read his blog because the free content Brian provides will help your new business in all kinds of ways. Copyblogger. com has an amazing content marketing course. The bigger bonus is that it's free. Visit: *www.copyblogger.com/content-marketing/*. To be clear, I am not an affiliate of Copyblogger.com nor am I receiving compensation for sending people to their site. I am merely a believer in the high value and excellent content that Brian and his team provide. Sign up for free updates on Copyblogger.com: *https://my.copyblogger.com/free-membership/*.)

Content marketing is the creating and sharing of valuable free content to attract and convert prospects into customers, and current customers into repeat buyers. The type of content you share is closely related to what you sell; in other words, you're educating people so that they know, like, and trust you enough to do business with you. This concept probably sounds familiar because it is similar to what Cialdini discusses in his book. People tend to do business with people they like, trust, and see as an authority. They also tend to do business with people who have taken the time to educate them on a particular product or service.

Done correctly, content marketing does three things:

1. It establishes you as an expert in your targeted niche (you have authority).

2. It educates your current and prospective customers by providing important information in their industry (you encourage reciprocation).

3. It provides your current and prospective customers with piece of mind because they know, like, and trust you to provide quality service or products (you are liked).

Your company and the experiences your customers have with it, define your brand. When customers engage you and you provide them with information that is useful to them, they will be happy to come back because they had a favorable experience. More importantly, providing high-quality information and resources to a potential customer raises the bar of experience. In addition, your customer will think, *If he/she is giving me this information for free, I can only imagine how good the paid information is!*

People do not want to be sold, even if you are selling them what they came to buy. They want to be in control of the buying decision. I was recently at a department store looking for a pair of shoes for a wedding I was attending. A sales associate immediately greeted me at the entrance of the men's department and asked if I needed any help or if he could show me anything specifically. I said, "No thanks, I'm okay—just looking around," even though I had a specific reason for being at the store. The sales associate did nothing wrong and was only being helpful according to his training. People who walk into stores are most likely interested in buying something, yet I instinctively rejected the sales associate's offer for help. The connection tends to be better through a story about an experience and education (again, content marketing).

People want valuable and useful information when they are making purchasing decisions. They do not want to be advertised, marketed, or sold to. Remember, people mainly spend money to solve a problem or achieve a desired result. Those businesses that can better help customers achieve that goal tend to sell the most. Think about your last big purchase: You probably didn't wait for an advertisement or commercial to persuade you to buy what you needed. You asked friends for referrals and checked online reviews on Amazon and CNET. Then you made the purchase. This is content marketing in a nutshell, and it leaves traditional advertising methods in the dust. Make no mistake—there is a method to sharing content, and it is not as easy just putting any old content on your Website. You have to do the work. Do not mistake content marketing for information marketing or "here's all of this useless information" marketing. People see through that and their bullshit meter goes off. Your credibility, if you had any, erodes instantly.

Storytelling

So how do you share useful content with your audience and build your credibility with them? One way is to tell a story of how you came to this business, a personal and authentic experience of what brought you to where you are today. The story you share makes you relatable to the customer, and makes the customer realize that you are in the business of solving problems.

There is a psychological phenomenon called *transportation* that explains why a story is more compelling to the listener or customer. The best salespeople use storytelling to share their messages. In the November 2000 issue of the *Journal of Personality and Social Psychology*, Melanie Green and Timothy Brock researched the role of transportation in the persuasiveness of public narratives. (Source: Green, Melanie and Timothy Brock. *Journal of Personality and Social Psychology*, Vol 79 (5), Nov 2000, 701–721.)

Transportation is defined as a mechanism used to get the listener absorbed in a story. Transportation also entails imagery, affect, and attentional focus. *Attentional focus* is a person's ability to choose what to pay attention to and what to ignore. In other words, people can get swept up into a story by relating to a character, and then be empowered to take action.

Do I just have to tell a story and the world will beat a path to my door? Of course not. It's about much more than just telling a story. It is important to tell a compelling story that brings customers into it and shows them why your product or service will solve their problem(s). The customer has to be able to relate to what you are saying. It is not an outlandish fairytale, but a realistic, true story. Your experience and your story have to be relatable and engaging to the listener.

In 2013, I spoke at the Ladies America—Women's Leadership Conference about small business and some of the concepts in this book. The opening keynote speaker was Sam Horn. Sam is the intrigue expert, a world-renowned author, keynote speaker, communications strategist, and executive coach who has trained some of the world's top entrepreneurs. Sam's keynote speech chronicled the importance of "speaking up and out" when sharing your experiences. She used the experience of her son applying for his dream job with NASA. During the application process, Sam's son failed to add a salient piece of experience he had while a student at Virginia Tech University. Sam skillfully leveraged the phenomenon of transportation in her speech, which drew the conference attendees in via vivid imagery and anecdotal examples.

I always use metaphors and analogies to illustrate the points I am trying to make in my speeches and presentations. For example, when speaking with a prospective client, I often share the importance of working with an experienced professional versus someone who is only moderately experienced, and how the difference can be disastrous if overlooked. I then use the following analogy in my story or presentation: As a frequent flyer, would you rather have a pilot who flies planes for a living, like Captain "Sully" Sullenberger (the pilot who successfully landed a U.S. Airways jet on the Hudson River after being struck by a flock of birds), or a pilot who is a weekend warrior and flies for fun? A less skilled pilot would have crashed the plane, just as a less skilled professional can crash your business.

Persuasive stories need to be engaging. Here are a few more factors that will make a story engaging and persuasive, these from another research study by Green and Brock titled *Persuasion: Psychological Insights and Perspectives* (Second Edition, 2005):

- Use literary techniques such as irony and metaphors to make the experience new and fresh.

- Imagery provides the listener or reader with visual story in her mind. She visualizes and "lives" the story as you share it.

- Suspense is obvious and keeps the attention of the listener or reader because she wants to know what happens next.

- *Modeling* involves presenting a character that the listener can relate to, follow, and emulate or copy. Sam's story about her son is a perfect example of modeling. You want your customer to realize that she can do the same thing as the character in your story or anecdote. Ideally, this character should go through the same kind of transformation that you want the reader or listener to go through.

In their book *Made to Stick*, Chip and Dan Heath reveal that stories are important in getting ideas to stick in the minds of listeners. For centuries, stories have been used to share ideas and explain important concepts. In the Bible, Jesus used parables (stories) containing metaphors and symbolism to explain important and complex concepts. According to a Copyblogger.com article by Brandon Yanofsky,

We humans process information much more efficiently when it's in the form of a story, and we're therefore much more likely to remember it. We quickly forget a dry recitation of the facts. If you want your marketing to really sizzle, if you want people to remember it, you need to turn your marketing messages into stories.

Your story should include the following three elements:

1. The problem

2. How you, your experiences, and your product can solve the problem

3. The solution

The basic principle is to tell your customers a story that allows them to experience what you are trying to share with them. For more on this, read Brandon's full article on Copyblogger.com: *www.copyblogger.com/storytelling-marketing/*.

The Science of Persuasion

The words you use in your stories and marketing materials will obviously play a large role in getting customers to buy from you. There are five words Gregory Ciotti believes are the most persuasive words in the English language, and which should be used in your headlines and marketing copy:

1. **You:** People will pay more money for personalization. This applies to e-mails, interaction, and conversation.

2. **Free:** Everyone likes free especially if value has been established in your product or offering. The customer must see that there is value in what you are offering for free.

3. **Because:** Cialdini says that people are more likely to adhere to a request if a reason is given for the request. Give your customers reasons to buy from you!

4. **Instantly:** People like to receive items they have purchased right away. In other words, Instant Gratification is important.

5. **New:** People like new things. Drive by an Apple store the day before a new version of the iPhone is released—people will literally camp out waiting for the pleasure of shelling out

$500-plus to get the new phone, even though they can wait a few weeks to get it.

Your stories should also do the following:

- Tell people specifically what you want them to do. This is also known as a *call to action*.

- Be appreciative of the feedback and engagement you receive from visitors and customers.

- Show how your solutions helped people without talking about yourself.

- Use testimonials in your offerings and marketing materials. Studies show that personalizing a testimonial with pictures and videos has a better result than without them.

- Provide a process for people to follow. Make it easy for a visitor or customer to understand what to do in order to buy from you.

Chapter 22
Social Media Marketing Tips

All companies need to market themselves. This is true for start-ups as well as established companies. However, there is a world of difference between offline marketing and online marketing. Let's start by looking at the more traditional methods of marketing.

- **Newspaper Advertisements (Online Ads):** One of the most effective methods of advertising is newspaper ads. Even in today's digital era, newspapers continue to be the most effective way of delivering content. When the digital era started, almost everyone expected newspapers to die a natural death. However, this medium has evolved and it is still alive and kicking. Today, you can download the e-versions of entire newspapers. These versions include all the news and advertisements published in the hard copy.

- **Banners and hoardings:** Take a walk or drive down any street in both urban and rural areas and you'll see banners and hoardings. These modes of advertising have been around for more than four decades. People predicted they would soon become extinct but, just like the newspaper, banners and hoardings have also evolved. The biggest change is the move from paper banners and hoardings to electronic and dynamic banners and hoardings.

- **Pamphlets and Flyers (Guerilla Marketing):** Open your mailbox and you'll find it stuffed with pamphlets. This is one of the most common and, surprisingly, one of the most effective methods of marketing. Consider this scenario: You clear your mailbox and shove all the pamphlets to one side. You scan through them and the various offers provided. Later in the week, you need a takeout restaurant's number. You'll probably find it in the heap of pamphlets!

While these methods have long been in use to market companies and their services, the advent of the social media platform added another dimension. Unfortunately, most entrepreneurs and business owners do not know how to tap this platform's potential. So let's start with some basic definitions.

- **Blog:** The basic definition of a blog is an online article. Another way to look at a blog is an online version of a newspaper article. Anyone and everyone can write a blog. The skill sets needed to write a blog are a good command of the English language, and a basic idea on how to give a structure to the blog. You can also find freelance writers for your blog posts on Freelancer.com.

- **Ranking:** This refers to the rank given to a Website by a search engine. The ranking will eventually decide what the visibility of the Website is. Websites or blogs with a high ranking will be found in the first few pages of a search. In contrast, Websites or blogs with low rankings will show up several pages in.

- **Traffic:** Traffic refers to the number of people visiting a Website. This is a major factor in the ranking of any Website. Search engines give better rankings to Websites with high volumes of traffic.

- **SEO:** This stands for Search Engine Optimization. There are many search engines on the Web. Google is mainly what matters in terms of how you are ranked. All these search engines run programs to rank a blog or a Website. SEO is a method in which the person writing the blog *optimizes* the content to ensure a good ranking on all the search engines.

- **Keywords:** One of the most common ways to optimize your content is thought the use of keywords. For example, an article on bank loans can use keywords such as "personal finance" and "loans" to ensure that the link shows up on the search engine when these words are used.

- **White Hat and Black Hat:** This refers to techniques used for optimizing content. White hat techniques are approved techniques that boost a Website's ranking. Black hat techniques are illegal ways of boosting ranking.

- **Back Links:** Back links are links that point back to your Website or blog. These could include links included in blogs or advertisements.

- **PPC:** PPC, or Pay Per Click, refers to social media advertising. You are paying for a certain number of people to click on your advertisement. The site will remove the advertisement once the limit has been reached.

The term "online business" was virtually nonexistent a decade ago. There were few companies that offered their services online, but consumers still preferred to visit actual brick-and-mortar locations. The only models that depended on a "semi-virtual" business environment were takeaway services and banks that offered customer service via the phone. While most people looked at this platform from a personal point of view, the business world saw its huge potential for business. Suddenly, business owners had a way of connecting to hundreds and even millions of customers. This platform removed all the restrictions associated with a normal brick-and-mortar store. Companies were no longer restricted by permits or timings. They could service customers of all ages and from all over the world.

The Internet made it easier for retailers to reach millions of people without having to spend millions of dollars. My goal here is to provide you with guidance and advice on a variety of social media platforms for your business. As of this writing, the important platforms are:

- Facebook
- YouTube
- Twitter
- LinkedIn

In the next few chapters I'll provide detailed information on the various business tools available on each of these platforms, as well as instructions on how to set up and operate a business on each. My ultimate aim is to introduce the power of social media to your business.

Chapter 23
Facebook

The first step to creating a presence on Facebook is to create a page for your company or service. In order to do this, go to *www.facebook.com*. Many of you probably already have a Facebook page for personal use, but I wanted to make sure I included a complete guide for your business.

1.   Next, click on the option **Create a Page**. This will take you to the next page.

2.   Next, click on any one of the six options available and fill in all the required details.

3.   Select a name for the page, and add a logo and a business statement. All of these should reflect your core business.

4.   Add a cover photo and click **Create a Page.**

Tip: If the name selected does not match the guidelines in Facebook, then the site will suggest a correction. You can accept the correction or click on the **Learn More** option to understand what are the options allowed. You cannot use any abusive words or proprietary names. The name of the page has to be spelled properly and cannot include symbols. Also, keep your page name short. Also, you can use your personal Facebook account to create a business page. In such a situation, your personal page will be your "landing" page. You can see your business page by clicking on the gear icon on the top right hand side of the page.

How to Generate Free Traffic

Now that you have published your page, you have to tell people about the page. The best way to do this is to inform your friends and family. This can be done in one of two ways:

1.   **Invite all your contacts on Facebook to view the page:** The first way to invite all your contacts is to click on the **Share** option. This option will post the page on your timeline. By using this

method, all your contacts will be able to see the page. You can also invite your contacts manually. In order to do this, click the option **Invite Your Friends**. This option will be displayed under the header "Build your audience," or on the right hand side of your page. The first option is much less tedious because everyone in your contact list can see the page. However, if you only want a handful of your contacts to view the page, you can manually select them using the **Invite Your Friends** option.

2. **Invite all your e-mail contacts to view the page:** Facebook allows you to share the page with all your e-mail contacts. In order to do this, click on **Build Your Audience**. Next, click **Invite All Your Email Contacts**. Next, select the e-mail service you want to use. Once you click on **Agree**, remember to click on the box next to "I am authorized to send invitations to the email addresses I've imported."

Now that you have the basic structure of the page and you've invited your friends and contacts to view the page, let's get an understanding of the various parts of the page.

Optimization and Page Management

Ostensibly, the next step is advertising. However, there is one step that comes before this that most people ignore: optimizing the page. Why is optimization important? The content on your page is still in its infancy. Remember, the people who have visited and liked your page are your friends, relatives, and acquaintances. Their motive is to encourage you and motivate you. Therefore, if you have 10 people who like your page, you should count it as only two people. Let me share a little secret with you: The best and simplest way to make your page popular is through its content. Later in this book, I will share various methods and tools for advertising, but these methods and tools will work well only if your content is good. Hence the maxim, "Content is king!" Of course, SEO and keywords need to be included while writing your content, but for now let's see how can we optimize and manage your page.

On the Admin Panel page you can edit all the content on your page. Here's how:

1. First click on **Edit Page** and select the **Update Page Info** option.

2. Next, click the **Edit** option next to **Topics**.

3. Click the **Edit** option next to the header **Long Description**. Mention more details about your page. Here you can use keywords related to your business to optimize your page. (Tip: Use a search engine and locate the appropriate keywords.)

4. Fill in all the remaining fields on this page. This is an important step. Facebook will display all the updated information on your main page.

Now that you have entered all the details about your company, you can post content. There are a few things to keep in mind when posting content on Facebook:

- **Keep it relevant:** The content you post should be relevant to the business. For example, if you are running a real estate business, sentences such as "Low rentals in new building near ABC Street" will attract followers.

- **Add links and visual content:** If you want to add a link or a photo or video, Facebook provides you separate options for the same.

- **Decide whom to share it with:** Sharing content is different from sharing the page. There are only two options here— **Everyone** and **Customize**. If you select **Everyone**, the content will be shared with everybody in your contact list. If you select **Customize**, you can select the specific Facebook users who will be able to see the content.

More tips:

Tip 1: Keep your content between 100 to 250 characters. This is the ideal length to capture people's attention.

Tip 2: Use visual aids such as photos and videos to generate more visitors.

Tip 3: Get 30 likes from your friends to unlock the **Insights** option. This option will tell you the ideal time to post content.

Creating and Managing Advertisements

Now we come to the most important section of the guide—Facebook advertisements. We will start with the basics and then progress toward the various advertising tools provided by Facebook. All advertisements on Facebook fall under the PPC (pay per click) model or the CPC (cost per click) model. Entrepreneurs and business owners tend to confuse them; but the reality is that they are different sides of the same coin. PPC is used as a general term, whereas CPC is used to define the daily budget needed for the advertising campaign.

Page promotion

1. The first step to advertise your page is to use an option called **Promote Page**. Most business owners prefer this option because it helps them reach a larger audience. It also helps them get new customers and build a bigger audience for their brand.

2. Once you click this button, you'll be asked to specify your budget.

3. Next, select your target audience.

4. Then add a funding source.

5. Once the payment is made, you're done!

Contrary to popular belief, Page Promotion is not the only method of advertising your content on Facebook. Here's how to create an advertisement on Facebook.

Ad creation

1. On your Facebook page, click the **Gear** icon on the top right-hand side of the page.

2. Next, click **Advertise On Facebook**. This will bring you to the an ad creation page.

3. Then click on the option **Create An Ad**. You will have to enter a URL, which can be your page or someone else's page.

4. The **Promote Page Posts** option is similar to promoting your page. However, now you are promoting only certain content on your page. Tip: By checking the box next to "Keep my ad up-to-date by automatically promoting my most recent post," you are telling Facebook to prioritize the latest content on the page. Hence,

your most recent content gets priority over the rest. If you want to promote only certain content, however, then you should uncheck this option.

5. Click on the **Get More Pages Likes** option. You will be asked to select a headline, a text or body, the landing view, and what stories should be shown.

6. Click on the type of advertisement you want and then scroll down. Alternatively, click **Advanced Options** and then scroll down. (Tip: If you click on **Advanced Options** and nothing pops up, don't panic. All you have to do is scroll down a bit farther.) There are two parts in the **Advanced Options**: the first is **Create Your Audience**, and the second is **Campaign, Pricing, and Schedule**.

Create Your Audience:

▶ First, select your country or city, age, and gender parameters. You can also decide the range of the city limits and whether you want an exact age match or not.

▶ Select the categories of the people you want to target.

▶ Choose the connections you want to target. You can choose anyone—people connected to your business or people not connected to your business.

▶ The advanced connection targeting helps you fine-tune the target audience. Ideally, these fields should not be filled out, but if you want to customize your audience even further, click the option **See Advanced Targeting Options**.

▶ Leave the Languages and Workplaces options blank.

Campaign, Pricing, and Schedule:

▶ First, start with the account settings and select your currency, country, and time zone. Remember these settings cannot be changed once the advertisement is published.

▶ Next, select the name of the campaign and the budget. There are two options: select how much you want to spend daily, or how much you want to spend during the entire campaign. Based on the budget option chosen, you will have different options when it comes to the schedule.

▶ Once you have selected the budget, select the optimal options. There are three optimization options to choose from:

> **Optimize for Likes**, **Optimize for Clicks**, or **Optimize for Impressions**. (Tip: Under **Optimize for Clicks**, you can select either the "Automatically optimize my budget to get more clicks" or the "Manually bid for clicks" option. Your final pricing will depend on the option selected.)

▶ Click on the **Review Ad** button.

▶ If you are happy with the advertisement, you can click **Place Order**. If not, go back and edit your Ad. Once you place the order, click **Add a Funding Source** for payment.

▶ Click on **Continue** and you will be asked to enter your payment information.

All advertisements submitted from Monday to Friday take 24 to 36 hours to be approved. Facebook will send you an e-mail either approving your advertisement or declining it. All advertisements have to comply with the rules and regulations posted by Facebook. You can view all the guidelines fine print here: *www.facebook.com/ad_guidelines.php.*

Before you publish your ad, review this checklist and make sure that:

☑ The profile photo is clear and measures 32 x 32 inches.

☑ The first 90 characters capture the most important point(s).

☑ All thumbnails (photos and/or videos) are clear and not blurred.

☑ The content relates to your business.

☑ The message is creative and innovative.

☑ People have to like the content to share it.

☑ Your target audience selection is correct.

☑ Your advertisement can get new customers.

☑ Facebook promotes your newest content 90 percent of the time.

Posts, Photos, and Videos: Some Do's and Don'ts
Posts

The main reason to post is to engage your audience and increase brand visibility.

◼ If you have a dedicated Web page for your brand, use your Facebook content to direct people to that Web page.

▶ Do not add the link to your post directly, but use the **Link** option to add the same.

▶ Use new features like hash tags (#word) to highlight content.

▶ Increase the level of interaction by posing questions related to your brand. Make sure your brand name is included in those questions.

Photos

Photos are used by brands to highlight their products.

▶ Always use a square image to maximize the usage of space.

▶ All photos used should belong exclusively to your brand. Don't use copyrighted or third-party images.

▶ Photos should be fun and engaging.

▶ Create an album or host your photo on Facebook.

▶ Allow customers to upload photos related to the brand.

▶ Don't add too many words to the photo.

Videos

Videos are the ultimate engagement medium on Facebook.

▶ A video should not be less than 20 seconds or more than three minutes.

▶ Videos should be related to the brand being promoted.

▶ Encourage participation by allowing your customers to upload videos related to the brand.

▶ Don't add too many words to the video.

▶ Always review all videos and photos submitted to prevent any violation of Facebook's policies.

Facebook Tools

So what tools does Facebook provide to business owners? Following are some essential tools you should know about and use.

Insights

This tool is extremely helpful to business owners. It uses the parameters set during the customer selection to display detailed information on the performance of the page. Hence, business owners have access to different parameters. Some of these parameters are:

- **Performance of content:** You can check the response to all the content posted by you on your page.

- **Demographic breakdown:** You can check the gender, age, country/city, and language breakdown of your visitors. This is very helpful when you are trying to reach out to a particular demographic.

- **Page views:** You can check the number of overall visitors and first-time visitors under the header **Reach**.

- **Frequency views:** You can check the number of times the page has been visited during a week. Available under the **Reach** header, you can also see a daily breakdown.

- **Hash tags:** This tool is not new to social media, but it's relatively new to Facebook. A hash tag, or #, is used to highlight a particular word. For example, if you want to highlight the word *burger*, you can add # *(yourbrandname) burger*. This will link the word to your brand's Webpage. Hash tags are a great method of cross-platform advertising.

- **Scheduling your posts:** This new feature from Facebook allows you to time your publications. You can now decide when content should show up on Facebook. If you time it with any other promotional activities, it will enhance visibility for your brand.

- **Unpublished posts:** This is another new feature that enables you to ensure that your content is shown only on the pages of certain Facebook users and not with all your Facebook friends.

As you can see, Facebook remains an important part of the social media platform. What makes it even more desirable for businesses is its wide variety of tools and constant innovations to help brand promotions. I've shown you the basics on how to create your page and market it. Once you have your page up and running, however, it is important to monitor the content. The best way to do this is to explore the various tools offered by Facebook. Your primary focus should be about engaging your customers. You can always learn the advanced features Facebook offers at a later date.

Chapter 24

LinkedIn

For various reasons, Facebook still has a more personal, intimate feeling to it. For a business owner who is just establishing his or her business, a professional profile is a must. Most importantly, business owners need to create a network to grow. This is exactly why LinkedIn was created.

Here's how to set up a company profile on LinkedIn:

1. Start by logging into *www.linkedin.com*. Once you enter the site, the sign in or sign up page shows up.

2. There are two options available to you. You can create your new profile or you can import your settings from Facebook. If you click the option **Sign Up With Facebook**, the first four fields will fill up automatically and you only have to enter the password.

3. Once you click **Continue**, you will be directed to create your company profile page.

4. Select your country by clicking on the drop down.

5. Next, enter your postal code.

6. Select the option **Employed**.

7. Enter your job title and tick the option "I am self employed." The **Company** field will change to **Industry**.

8. Select your industry and click on **Create My Profile**.

9. Add your e-mail address and password and click **Continue**. LinkedIn will look for people from your address book already registered on the site. It will then recommend that you connect with these individuals.

10. Select the people whom you want to add and click **Add Connection(s)**.

11. You can add the link to your Facebook page and your Twitter account.

12. Select one of two plan options: the Basic plan, which is absolutely free, or the Premium plan, which as of this writing starts at 24.95 USD. LinkedIn will highlight the plan that is best for you. (Note: LinkedIn will bill you for a period of one year.)

13. Click on **Review Order** and your account will be upgraded.

14. Before you proceed, make sure you confirm your e-mail address. (Once you enter your e-mail address, you will get a confirmation e-mail from LinkedIn. You will need to confirm your address to unlock the full power of LinkedIn.)

Improve Your Profile

Now that we have created your company's profile, the next step is to improve it. You can use the profile as you have created it, but its impact will be severely limited.

1. To edit your profile, click **Profile** and then **Edit Profile**.

2. On the Edit page, add a logo of your company or brand.

3. Next, click **Edit Contact Info**. Click on the pen/pencil icon to add or change the content in the relevant fields.

Options

LinkedIn differs from other sites in that it recommends which options you should fill in. Click on each of the recommended options to fill them.

1. **Experience:** Here you should fill out your entire work experience through the present. Include any roles you held in companies other than your own. You can include as many companies as you wish. Click on the **Save** option after you add each company.

2. **Education:** Add all your educational qualifications. Click **Save** after each one.

3. **Skills:** This is one of the most important parts of your profile. This section will highlight all your strengths and skill sets. You can add up to 50 skills. Typing in the first few words will prompt the list to come up.

4. **Summary:** In this section, you can add the link to your Website. You can also submit videos, photos, and write-ups related to your brand.

Tips to remember while uploading a file

The file should not exceed 100 megabytes. If you are uploading a presentation, these are the extensions allowed: .pdf; .ppt; .PPS; .pptx; .ppsx; .pot; potx; and .odp. If you are uploading a document, it must one of the following: .Pdf; .Doc; .Docs; .rtf; or .Odt. If you are uploading images, these are the extensions allowed: .png; .GIF; .JPEG; .JPG.

Groups and Networking

The core strategy of any business owner and entrepreneur is to develop his or her brand by networking. In the real world, this includes becoming a member of various groups, meeting and discussing strategies with individuals from your industry, taking part in discussions and enrolling in forums, and so on. LinkedIn replicates this model in the virtual world. LinkedIn has combined the entire process of networking under the headers **Network** and **Interests**. The options under the Network tab are Contacts, Connections, and Alumni.

Contacts

This refers to all the people whom you have connected with on LinkedIn. This could include friends, relatives, and business contacts. Because all the connections are filed under one header, it is an organized and effective way to manage all your contacts. LinkedIn allows you to see how many friends, colleagues, members of groups, partners, and classmates are part of your group.

Connections

LinkedIn allows you to add connections from all your e-mail addresses, including the e-mail address you registered with, your contacts from Gmail, Yahoo, Outlook, and Hotmail, and any other e-mail address you use, such as a work e-mail. The best part about this feature is that every time you add a contact, you can check if they are a part of LinkedIn; if not, you can send them an e-mail from LinkedIn asking them to connect with you, like so:

1. Once you click on the **Agree** option, LinkedIn will first show you all those who are a part of LinkedIn.

2. Once you click **Add Connections** or **Skip This Step**, LinkedIn will then show the details of those individuals who have not yet joined.

3. Select the people whom you want to invite and send an invitation.

Alumni

Your friends from school and college are valuable sources of information. LinkedIn recognizes this and allows you to connect with them. If you click **Find Alumni**, LinkedIn will display the page you need. You can then search by location, company name, and area of expertise, and interests to find and connect with anyone from your student days.

The options under the **Interests** tab are **Companies**, **Groups**, and **Influencers**.

Companies

Using this link, you can follow certain companies and brands. They may be related to your line of work, the sector you work in, sectors you want to get work from, or companies you admire. LinkedIn will also recommend companies that you should follow. However, this is the step where you can also add your company details.

On the top right-hand side of your page is an option called **Add Company**. Enter the name of your company and your official e-mail address. Click the box next to "I verify that I am the official representative of this company and have the right to act on behalf of my company in the creation of this page," and click **Continue**. This will create your company's page on LinkedIn.

Groups and Influencers

This is one of the biggest and most influential links available on LinkedIn. This is the best option when it comes to networking. Under this option, you can select which groups you want to be a part of. For example, if you are from the real-estate sector, you can join groups made by buyers and sellers, or groups made by real-estate companies or agents. When you join a group, it is reflected in your profile. LinkedIn also allows you to create a group and invite your connections to join the group. Here's how:

1. Click the link called **Create a Group**.

2. Select the logo or cover phone. Click on the box next to "I acknowledge," enter a group name, and select the type of the group.

3. Enter the brief description of the group followed by more detailed information.

4. Enter the link of your Website and the e-mail of the person creating the group.

5. You can decide if people require your permission to join or can join automatically. You can also choose if you want to show this group in the general directory, and whether members can show the logo of the group on their profiles.

6. Decide if you want to send an update to your connections about the creation of the group.

7. Decide whether members can invite others to join the group.

8. Enter the content of the e-mail message sent out on approval.

9. Select the default language option (it is always set to English).

10. If the group is catering to people from one location, select the location option; this will allow you to choose the country and the postal code.

11. Click the box next to "Check to confirm you have read and accept the Terms of Service."

12. Your final decision will be whether it is an "open drop" or a "member only" group. Everyone can see open group discussions, whereas member group discussions can be seen only by members. With so much control allowed, you can easily see why the Groups forum is the most influential forum on the Website.

Influencers

The aim of LinkedIn is to help you grow your business and educate you. With this in mind, LinkedIn offers you something called **Influencers**. Under this link, you will find influential businesspeople as well as world-famous personalities (for example, Deepak Chopra). Based on your profile, LinkedIn will show you which influencers you should follow. Once you subscribe to any of these influencers, their daily updates will reflect on your profile page.

Advertising

So you've created your company's profile on LinkedIn. You've joined and created groups, and even subscribed to certain influencers. But the big question, of course, is just how to promote your business on LinkedIn. LinkedIn actually allows you to target and connect with other professionals. Unlike Facebook, here your entire audience is made up of people who run their own businesses or who are a part of the corporate workforce. Hence, you are reaching out to CEO's, managers, and employees all at the same time. LinkedIn allows you to target your audience by their title, nature of the job, their industry, the size of their organization, and where they are on the corporate ladder. You can decide if you want to pay by clicks or impressions, and determine the timeline of the advertisement. There are no long-term contracts or commitments when you advertise on LinkedIn. Finally, LinkedIn gives you the freedom to decide on the type of advertisement you want to use. You can choose a combination of text and visual ads, or choose to post video ads or text-only ads.

Creating an ad

Before you create an advertisement, you have to convert your individual account to a business account. Here's how:

1. Click on your name on the top right-hand corner of the page and select **Create a Business Account**.

2. Enter the company name (created earlier), the account name, and the billing currency.

3. You'll see two options: **Creating an Ad** and **Sponsor an Update**. With **Creating an Ad** you can create a brand-new advertisement that is comprised of text, visuals, and/or video.

4. When you click on this option, enter the name of the campaign, the language, and the type of ad: Select **Basic** for text and images, and **Video** for video campaigns.

5. Decide whether the customer should be taken to your brand's Website or to your profile on LinkedIn.

6. If you have an image, you can add it or you can add a video. Enter the headline and a two-line description.

7. With the **Sponsor an Update** option, you can promote any update posted on your profile. When you click on this option, all you have to do is enter the name of the campaign and select which update you want to promote. The language field and the company field are autopopulated.

Audience Selection

Next, we will look at the various parameters for audience selection:

1. Once you click the **Next** button for either the new ad or sponsored update, you will see the basic option available for audience selection. You start by selecting the target location of your ad. When you click inside the text box, LinkedIn will show you options for all the continents across the world. Select your desired location from the options available.

2. Next, select the organizations or companies you wish to target. You can select all companies registered on the Website by clicking **All**, you can choose by name by clicking **By Name**, or you can choose by industry and company size by clicking **By Category**.

3. Check the box that enables you to reach LinkedIn members on other Websites through the LinkedIn Audience Network. This allows your advertisement to be displayed on all Websites that show LinkedIn ads.

Let us take a quick peek at some of the other targeting options available. As you can see, barring the age field, the **All** option is selected by default in all the other options.

Pricing and final payment

Once you have selected your parameters and you click **Next**, LinkedIn will take you to the Pricing page. Like all other social media platforms, LinkedIn bills you on a CPC (cost per click) basis. There are two payment options: pay for every click, or pay every time the ad is displayed. LinkedIn will show you the minimum amounts for your currency by default.

1. Select your daily budget (again, the minimum budget is suggested by LinkedIn) and then select how long you want your advertisement to run for.

2. The final option to select is **Lead Collection**. By clicking this, you will turn on the lead collection feature. Once you click on **Save Changes**, LinkedIn will take you to the Payment page.

3. Once you enter the payment details, click on **Review Order**. All advertisements take around 24 hours to show up on the Website. Make sure you review all the guidelines and associated fine print online.

Tools Provided By LinkedIn

We have already seen that advertisements are powerful. However, the LinkedIn advantage does not end here. LinkedIn offers company page owners a number of tools. Here are a couple of the latest, as of this writing:

- **Percentage of Engagement:** This option shows you the total percentage of interactions, clicks, and people following you (in layperson's terms, all the people who have seen your updates and have interacted with you). You can check the content and the audience selection, as well as the date and time options to boost your popularity even further.

- **Percentage of Demographics:** On the basis of your target audience, you can check details such as age group, size of organization, and roles or functions of people, and understand which demographic is being impacted the most from your posts. This will help you modify your content to reach your chosen demographic even more effectively.

- **Comparison:** LinkedIn now includes a comparison of all similar pages. This allows companies to see how other company pages in their sector are performing. It helps set the bar high and drives companies to aim for better performance.

■■■

We have only touched on the immense power of LinkedIn. My recommendation is to set up your account as soon as possible. Once your advertisements are up and running, you can become familiar with all the tools LinkedIn gives you access to.

Chapter 25
YouTube

Started in February of 2005, YouTube has grown to be a global phenomenon. Part of the Google family, the Website today caters to millions of viewers. The rise of the social media platform has pushed the popularity of YouTube even further. Hence, this makes it an important platform for any business, including your own. Let's start with a step-by-step process on how to create a YouTube account:

1. Visit *YouTube.com* in your browser.

2. Click **Sign In**. If you have a Google account, you automatically have a YouTube account as they are synched. If you have a Gmail ID, you can log in using that ID and password. If not, you can click on **Create an Account** (on the top right hand side). Once you fill out all the required fields and click **Next Step**, your account is ready to use. This is your default page.

As you probably know, YouTube works exclusively on videos. Hence, there are three basic features for every account. The first option is **Categories**. When you click on **Browse Categories**, you will be shown categories such as Animation or Automotive, for example. You can choose videos from any category depending on your needs. When you choose videos, it will then take you to the next step, **Channels**. You can choose to make your subscriptions private or public. Once you click **OK**, the subscribed channel will show up on the left-hand side of your home page.

Now that you have an account and are familiar with some of the basic features, we will explore how to advertise content and attract customers. Before we go into details, let us first look at some basic tips to get you started.

Most newcomers to the YouTube platform know that advertising on the platform is through a visual medium. However, they fail to really harness the power of this medium because they fail to take a few necessary preliminary steps first:

- **Analyze existing videos:** Start by going through various advertisement videos on YouTube. Check out videos from various channels. This will give you a general idea about the themes and basic methods followed by advertisers.

- **Understand the use of keywords:** The use of keywords is as important on YouTube as it on the other social media sites. Try various tools to find relevant keywords for your business and include them in the descriptions and tags for your videos.

- **Use the best thumbnails:** Remember that a thumbnail is a preview of the video. To select the best preview, go to your account setting in **My Accounts**, select the video, and click on **Edit**. Using the right thumbnails will help attract more customers.

- **CTAs, or Calls to Action:** These are the means by which you can interact with viewers. Requests such as "Please share your thoughts" and "Please rate this video" are the most commonly used CTAs on YouTube.

- **Do not impose:** Most advertisers make the mistake of making high-pressure sales pitches. The successful ones act as guides. They handhold potential buyers and show them the value of the services they offer.

How to Make Your Video Advertisement

This process can be easily divided into the following steps: plan, shoot, edit, and publish.

Planning

Let's start with the planning process. In order to make an impact on your audience, you need to tell a great story through the video. Hence, your planning process will begin with choosing a strategy and the corresponding approach. When you are writing the strategy, you should decide on the target audience, the services you are going to promote, what you think the audience is going to look for in that service or product, and your final goal.

The next step in the planning process is writing the script. Because most of us are amateurs at this, we have to divide the script into three parts. An introduction (by you or someone representing you) starts by giving a brief introduction to the service being advertised. Next, explain how your service differs from others and its USP (unique selling proposition). Finally, close the video with a CTA (call to action), such as "Tell us your common recurring home repair problems" or "Visit our Website to check out our services and rates."

Next, you should decide on your approach. Because it is a video platform, you have to come up with an innovative method. For example, if you are promoting a home repair business, you could come up with small videos to show viewers how to make minor repairs to their homes. Make the video simple to understand and grasp. By adding your Website's link to the video, you will automatically guarantee more hits and traffic. You can check out more examples at [hyperlink] *www.YouTube.com/advertise* [hyperlink]. You should dedicate a minimum of two to three hours for the entire planning process.

Shooting the video

Next, let's look at the actual process of shooting the video. Before you begin, you need to conceptualize the entire process from start to finish. Start by deciding the sequence of events that will be shot. Take the example of the home repair business. Your first sequence could be someone making a quick introduction. (Tip: Don't shy away from using a good-looking member of the opposite sex. He or she can be a friend or a relative.) The next sequence might show the person doing an actual repair, such as fixing a leaky pipe. The third sequence could then introduce you as the person who taught him or her how to do it. The final sequence could be a CTA, such as "Visit ABC.com for all your home repair needs!"

Before they begin shooting, most entrepreneurs try to save money by doing the shot themselves or using friends or relatives who are amateur filmmakers. Please understand that this is not a family video, but a professional endeavor. A poorly shot video will defeat the entire purpose of the advertisement. However, if you still want to go ahead and shoot the video yourself, here are some crucial tips and caveats:

- ▶ The person doing the introduction should never be at the center of the frame, but standing just a little to the side.

- ▶ The video camera being used should be kept stable on a tripod.

- ▶ The background should be free of clutter. If you wish, you can shoot at your place of business, but make sure that the background looks neat and clean.

- ▶ Ask the presenter to maintain a normal and friendly tone. He or she should imagine that he/she is addressing friends.

- ▶ There should be no background noise at all. This will ensure that the commentary is clearly audible.

- ▶ Always use cue cards. This will ensure that the presenter knows what to say next. Tape cue cards to the bottom of the camera lens or use a free online teleprompter: *www.CuePrompter.com* or *www.FreeTele-prompter.com*.

- ▶ Always ensure that the presenter is within five feet of the microphone. It is preferable to use a video camera with an external mic input jack.

- ▶ Finally, don't keep zooming in and out. This will affect the quality of the sound. Shoot different sequences separately and then join them together when you edit the video. (Tip: Always have multiple shots of each sequence available. This will help you during the editing process.)

Editing the video

Once you have shot the video, the next step is editing it. Today, editing and putting videos together is a snap. YouTube makes it even easier by offering a built-in video editor. To access the video editor, click on the word **Upload** on the top right-hand side. You'll be directed to the video editor's page. The editing features offered by YouTube are as follows:

- ■ Combining videos
- ■ Adding music to the videos
- ■ Trimming clips to make them shorter
- ■ Stabilizing clips
- ■ Adding text effects and transitions

YouTube offers you a database of 250 free music tracks to use. Remember, you can only use music clips that are rights-free or copyrighted by you. Try not to experiment with features like transitions and text effects. You can, however, add one or two effects, such as text containing your phone number and Website address. Once you finish editing, please ensure that you save it in one of the following formats: .mp4; .mov; .avi; .wmv; .3gpp; .mpegps; or .flv.

Publishing the video

Publishing your video is simple, too:

1. Click on the word **Upload** on the top right hand side of the site.

2. Click the arrow to upload your video. This can take a long time, depending on the size of the file. YouTube will optimize the file to ensure that it is optimized for streaming.

3. The next step is to add a title, a description, and tags. The title should have the keywords right at the beginning and your brand name at the end.

4. Market the video using the description column. A good description will read something like this: "Discover the all-new collection of women's watches at Vera Simon!"

5. The next step is the addition of tags. Tags in layperson's language are words that search engines use to display your video. You can use the tools available online to understand keywords related to your business and then add them in the tags column.

6. Decide which category your video falls into. Click on the **Category** option on the right-hand side on the screen. Once you choose the category and select the option **Public** below it, YouTube will process the video and show you three thumbnails. Select the best thumbnail for your video. Once you select the thumbnail, save your options. Your video is now ready to be shown to the world!

Using Google AdWords to Promote Your Video

We are now going to the marketing section. The best marketing tool provided by Google and YouTube is Google AdWords. Google AdWords is a highly successful advertising program that uses Google and all its partner Websites to increase visibility for your product or service. Here's how to set up your Google AdWords account:

1. Log in to *adwords.google.com/video*. This will first ask for your Gmail password and then bring you to the **Time Zone and Currency** page.

2. Next, select your country, time zone, and currency. These can be set up only once. Then click **Continue**. You will be directed to the AdWords account page.

3. Click on the link **Sign in to Your AdWords Account**. You will be sent to the **Campaign** page. Click on the **Campaigns** tab to create your campaign.

4. Click on the option **Create Your first Campaign**. You will be directed to the editor page. Click on **Type** and **Select Online Video**. Selecting this option will bring you to the **Video Campaign** page. On the left-hand side of the page is an option called **Click on Linked YouTube Accounts**. Here are the fields you will need to fill in:

   ▶ **Campaign:** Type the name of your campaign.

   ▶ **Budget:** Enter the per-day amount you are willing to spend.

   ▶ **Delivery Time:** There are two options: **Standard** means the advertisement will be distributed evenly as per your budget; **Accelerated** means the advertisement will be shown as soon as possible.

5. Select the location where the advertisement will be shown and the language of the advertisement.

6. The next option can be used to directly link your advertisement from your YouTube account.

7. Finally, you'll come to the advanced options that have to be selected. Your first option is scheduling. Start by selecting a start date and an end date.

8. Next, decide when the advertisement should be shown. Click the **Edit** option.

9. Next there are three delivery options. Spread the advertisement evenly to get more views, or spread it evenly to get more leads. You can also select the third option to rotate it equally between these

two. You can also decide if you want to cap impressions or not—meaning that you can decide how many times one user sees the same advertisement.

10. The final option is to decide which devices can see the advertisements. The best option is to keep it on the default settings. (There is another option called **Mobile Bid** adjustments. Please leave this empty.) Click **Save** and **Continue**.

Decide your target audience

Now that you have chosen your parameters, you will have to choose your audience. Following are the parameters for audience selection:

1. Start by naming your target selection.

2. Next, select the maximum amount you are ready to pay for each view.

3. Select the demographics of the audience, the topics selected, and their interests. This allows for an extremely targeted campaign. (Experienced advertisers who know how and where to place their advertisements use the advanced options. You can ignore them.)

4. Target those who are looking for specific items or keywords. Select the keyword and click on **Add**. Click **Done** and then **Save Targeting Group**.

If your bid amount is more than your budget, you will have to decrease the bid amount. (Remember that the budget was set up in the previous *step*.)

Set up the payment method

1. Start by selecting the country.

2. Choose the payment method.

3. Clicking on **Continue** will bring you to the **Terms and Conditions** page.

4. Provide the billing details, your address, and click **Save and Activate**. Once you do this, your advertisement is active.

   Tip: You can add your own CTA message to the video. Here's how:

5. Click on **Campaign** and then the video option on the left. Go to the video that will be used.

6. Click **Call to Action Overlay**.

7. Type in the headline, the description, and the URL.

Set up your channel

In order to make yourself visible to viewers, you will have to set up your channel. Your channel is your business center on YouTube. To access your channel settings, click on the blue square or the down arrow on the top right-hand side of the page.

1. Next, click **My Channel**.

2. To describe your channel, click on the **About** tab. You will see the option **Channel Description**. Click on the **+** arrow next to it and enter your channel description. You should include keywords as well as any additional details, such as the time for posting videos. Click **Done** once you have completed it.

3. Enter the overlay links that will be seen on your videos. To do this, click on the plus (**+**) arrow seen next to Links. Here you can enter the title and the URL of your Web page.

4. Add your icon and select channel art. Remember the blue square we talked about earlier? Now that gets replaced with your icon.

5. Click the blue square. You will see a small pen/pencil icon on the top right-hand side.

6. Click on **Edit** on Google+.

7. Click on the blue icon once more.

8. Add your logo and click on **Set as Profile Photo**. Remember that it will take some time to show up on YouTube.

9. Similarly, click on **Channel Art**.

10. Select a photo as a background. Your logo and photos should represent your business and brand.

11. Click on the **Down** arrow or the blue square and select **Video Manager**.

12. Now select your video and add tags (for example, jewelry, luxury watches, home repair) to your video. Congratulations—you are now up and running on YouTube!

YouTube Analysis Tools

Let us now look at the various tools offered by YouTube:

- **YouTube Watch:** Every advertisement uploaded by you will have a bar graph attached to it. (This will be seen only by you.) This graph will show you the performance of the video. If you click on the graph, you can see the number of people who have viewed the page, the rating, comments, and Favorites. You can also see the demographic breakdown of your audience.

- **YouTube Analytics:** Click on the arrow or your logo on the top right-hand side and select **Video Manager**. This will bring you to the Analytics page of YouTube. As you can see, this option gives you detailed information on the overall performance of all your videos. You can use this to check which of your videos are getting the best reviews and highest number of views. My suggestion to you is to click on each of the links on the left-hand side. This will give you much more detailed information and more insights into each video's performance.

- **AdWords Analysis:** Remember the Google AdWords campaign we set up? Here are a few insights that AdWords can give us:

  ▶ **Videos Tab:** You can see the number of views and the CTA performance of your campaign.

  ▶ **Targets Tab:** Here you can see what the audience performance was per your selection.

  ▶ **Ads Tab:** Here you can see the breakdown of impressions, views, and view rate.

  ▶ **Settings Tab:** You can change your budget and your target audience as per your requirements using this tab.

■■■

YouTube is the perfect visual platform for advertising. However, it will take some time for you to master it. Keep a close eye on your performance and make changes as and when necessary.

Chapter 26
Twitter

Twitter is a micro-blogging and social networking site. The unofficial credo of Twitter is that "less is better." While Facebook uses posts as its primary method of connection, Twitter uses Tweets. Every Tweet has a 140-character restriction, so users have to communicate within these parameters. So how does one set up a Twitter account?

1. Start by logging into *www.twitter.com*.

2. Enter your name, e-mail address, and password, and click on **Sign up for Twitter**.

3. Select the name by which you want to be seen and click on **Create My Account**. You will then be taken through a short tutorial.

4. You will be given option to follow local celebrities in your area. Select **Five** and click **Next**. You will be asked to follow five more people or organizations. Do that and click **Next**.

5. Add people from your contact lists.

6. Once you select the e-mail service, it will ask for access to your contact list and then display those who are already on Twitter.

7. Select the people you want to follow from the list shown and click **Next**.

8. The site will then ask you to invite people from your contact list to join you.

9. Next, upload your photo or logo and write a description about yourself or your business.

10. Once you have updated both, click on **Done**.

Set up Your Business on Twitter

Now that you have set up your account on Twitter, let's focus on setting up your business:

1. On the home page, scroll down to the section on the right-hand side of the page.

2. Click on the link **Businesses**.

3. Click on **Let's Go!** (Tip: If you select $0–5,000.00 USD, you will get the Self-Service account, If you select an amount greater than $5,000 USD, you will have the Full-Service account.) Then fill in the following information:

   ▶ First and last name.

   ▶ E-mail. This can be your personal e-mail or "official" e-mail address.

   ▶ Your Twitter username. Twitter assigns a handle starting with @ to your business. This must be a truncated name of your company.

   ▶ Company—the full name of your company.

   ▶ Website—the link to your company's Website.

   ▶ Industry—the sector to which your company belongs.

   ▶ Job Title—your position in the company.

   ▶ Job Function—your role in the company.

   ▶ Phone—your personal or office phone number.

4. Then click **Submit**.

5. Twitter will then review your information and then send you an e-mail invitation to advertise on the Website.

The Basics of Marketing on Twitter

Now that we have set up your account, we need to talk about marketing. Twitter allows you access to a large number of users. As of this writing, the Website receives 400 million Tweets a day and has close to 200 million active users. There are four things to keep in mind when it comes to marketing on Twitter:

1. **Take advantage of real-time connection:** The popularity of Twitter ensures that a wide number of topics are discussed on the site. This automatically includes companies and services offered by them. For example, someone who is unhappy with the service he received from a company can communicate that experience to millions in just a few words.

2. **Follow your competitors:** Remember the setup process. When you are asked to select the people or companies you want to follow, you can select your competition and start following them. This gives you valuable insights on what tactics are being employed by your competition. You can also follow CEOs and other industry leaders to gain valuable insights into the way they think.

3. **Use Twitter Ads to grow:** Twitter Ads is an extremely important business tool. This tool allows you to generate your own ads and gives you access to various analytical tools. You can connect with consumers through exciting advertisements using the previous option. We will discuss this in greater detail later in this chapter.

4. **Check out marketing strategies of other companies:** Twitter as a business platform offers companies a wide variety of marketing options. You can now check out the strategies of companies from other sectors and understand how to design and modify your advertisements for the greatest impact. Click **Here** for some success stories.

The Basics of Tweeting

In order to understand the Twitter platform better, you need to become conversant in some of the basic terminology used in this platform:

- **Tweet:** A Tweet is the basic format of messaging on Twitter.

- **Re-Tweet:** On Facebook or YouTube, posts and videos are shared using the Share function. However, in Twitter, Re-Tweet is the term used when a message has been shared.

- **Hash tags:** Twitter is the original inventor of the hash tag (#). The hash tag was invented to help users mention companies or services in their messages. It tells users that a Tweet is connected to a particular company.

- **The @ sign:** Twitter was also the first platform to use the @ sign extensively. Every user is assigned a handle using the @ sign. This allows users to reference themselves in their messages. This is called a "mention." The handle can also be used to send a DM (direct message). For example, if you want to Tweet a customer named Ronaldo C., you can send a DM in this format: "@Ronaldo C, please advise your tracking number." Similarly if you use the **Reply** button, the message will start with the @ sign.

You can view the entire list of Twitter terminology here:

https://support.twitter.com/groups/31-twitter-basics/topics/104-welcome-to-twitter-support/articles/166337-the-twitter-glossary#

Establishing Your Company on Twitter

Now that we have learned the basics, let's look at how to establish your company on Twitter. In order to do this, you first need to understand some basic rules:

- ▶ **Don't be formal:** Twitter is the ultimate definition of a social platform. While LinkedIn is a formal environment, Twitter is the opposite. For example, take this Tweet: *@PopChips: Grab life by the bags!* See how the company is grabbing attention by using an informal, even irreverent tone? This is so much better than saying "Buy our chips because they taste better"!

- ▶ **Give insights into your company:** Twitter is all about transparency. Consumers prefer companies they can relate to. This can be done by posting regular Tweets about your company that are authentic and either funny or informative. You can also include photos and videos about company events. Remember, the personal connection always works.

- ▶ **Be flexible while Tweeting:** A company's Tweets should be modified according to the situation. Let's say you are an airline company and you keep building followers with light-hearted Tweets and insights into new, lower fares. However, if a follower is facing a problem with the airline, the tone needs to be more formal and polite: @JetNew: We're very sorry about what you've been through. We do hope you will enjoy your free flight and can get some rest while in MCO.

- ▶ **Appreciate and address concerns immediately:** Twitter is a miniversion of the real world. In order to build more followers, you need to be quick to reply to Tweets, both positive ones as well as those that voice concerns or complaints.

Improve your Tweets

Continuing with the theme of establishing your company on Twitter, let us now look at how Tweets can be improved:

- **Think about frequency:** The biggest question facing companies is how often they should Tweet. Unfortunately, there is no easy answer for this. Many companies keep their followers interested with humorous Tweets and updates on daily activities. Depending on your business and number of followers, you might want to do the same.

- **Observe the rules of engagement:** The best way to build a followers list is to engage your readers. This can be done by using Tweets as a method of conversation and by posting high-quality content.

- **Use visual media:** People respond more to visual content. Twitter allows you to share content directly from other social media Websites. This will help you automatically advertise your brand across multiple platforms with just one click. Just by adding a photo, you can automatically gain publicity for your brand.

- **Your profile is your identity:** Most companies make the mistake of creating a weak profile. Your profile should be consistent throughout. Also, ensure that your profile is not design heavy, as it may not reflect properly on some mobile platforms.

- **Use Twitter along with other platforms:** We have already seen how good content is necessary for any profile. Similarly, you should make Twitter an integral part of all your campaigns across other platforms. This will help increase your number of followers.

- **Use exiting followers to promote:** You can incentivize your existing followers to promote you. For example, a coffee house might offer discounts on their products for the first 10 people who achieve 50 re-Tweets. By offering such incentives, the coffee house is gaining publicity without having to spend extra money.

- **Take advantage of collaborations and third-party applications:** Small-business owners can collaborate with each other for promotional activities. For example, a courier service owner can team up with the coffee house for cross-promotional activities. Twitter also offers third-party applications that can optimize content and get more followers for your brand.

■ **Get your employees involved:** Organizations should involve their employees for all their Twitter activities. By using your staff, you can ensure that your Twitter updates are more timely and interactive. It helps the staff connect with consumers and ultimately helps in brand loyalty.

All About Twitter Ads

Twitter Ads are the advertising programs offered by Twitter. Twitter has followed the lead of other social networking platforms that offer similar programs. While most of the other platforms offer the same types of advertising programs for all companies, Twitter differentiates itself by offering two different types of programs on the basis of company size. These advertising programs are called Twitter Ads Self Service and Twitter Ads Full Service. Let us look at the services that are offered by both programs.

■ **Promoted Accounts:** This option displays accounts that a particular user should follow. For example, if you mention technology as one of your interests, Twitter will "promote" certain relevant companies and indicate that you should follow them. This option is a great way to help people interested in your sector to discover your brand. It benefits the advertiser because it is an extremely targeted piece of advertising that narrows down the potential client base by matching interests and sectors.

■ **Promoted Tweets:** While the Promoted Accounts option highlights the advertiser, Promoted Tweets will highlight specific content. This option is used by companies to highlight offers concerning their services, build awareness about their brand, and promote events sponsored by them. By promoting an update, a brand is targeting those individuals who are looking for the particular service provided by the brand. This type of advertising is also seen in searches.

■ **Promoted Trends:** The first two options focused on the advertiser's account and his or her updates. In contrast, Promoted Trends focuses on the topics related to the advertiser. As an example, #SOAFX is being promoted, meaning that every time someone mentions #SOAFX in their Tweet, the **Promoted** tag will be attached. This ensures that the visibility for #SOAFX increases as compared to other topics. Hence, any advertiser can select a word connected to his or her business and use the Promoted Trends option to increase the overall visibility. This serves to highlight his or her service/product and help it stand out from the competition. (Note: Promoted Trends is only offered under the Full Service option on Twitter. This is decided based on the budget selected by you.)

How to set up an ad on Twitter

1. Click on **Start Advertising** or **Let's Go!**

2. The first option is to choose the location. Remember, these choices will coincide with the details given during the setup. Twitter will change the details of locations and currency depending on your **Country** selection.

3. You can select to advertise to all users, users in a specific country, or users in only certain countries. If you select the second or third options, you will have to manually enter the country details or details of the cities. Twitter will help you by suggesting names with its autofill function.

4. If your budget is more than $5,000 USD, Twitter will help you decide on your target audience. Twitter offers you a number of options in this regard:

    ▶ **Keywords:** You can target people based on their search patterns in Twitter. By using this option, the next time a keyword related to your business is used, people will be shown your Account or Tweet or Trend, as per your choice.

    ▶ **Interests:** By selecting this option, you can target Tweeters who have similar interests, or interests related to your industry.

> ▶ **Geography:** This is the first option selected when you decided the location in which you wanted to advertise.

> ▶ **Devices:** Because most people use Twitter with their smartphones, you can choose which smartphone manufacturer to target.

> ▶ **Gender:** In this option, you can choose which gender(s)— male or female or both—to target for your advertisements.

> ▶ **Similar to people following you:** If you already have a few followers, you can decide to target more people who have similar profiles.

5. Next, decide your budget to promote your account. You can decide how much you want to spend per day for Twitter to promote your account. Twitter will show you the minimum value to be entered. You can also choose to skip this option by clicking on **Skip for Now**. If not, click **Start Promoting Your Account**.

6. Decide on a per-day budget to promote your Tweets. Twitter also allows you to let it choose the Tweet; or, you can choose **Tweet to Promote**. You can choose to skip this option or you can click **Start Promoting Your Tweets**.

7. If you are using the **Self Service** option (the one recommended by Twitter for us based on the budget selected), you will have to choose one of the previous options. However, if Twitter gives you the Full Service option, you will be directed to the Promoted Trends option. The pricing structure is same as those for the previous two.

8. Select your method of payment.

9. Enter your credit card details, your billing address, and click on **Complete Setup to Start Advertising**.

Analytical Tools Offered by Twitter

Twitter Self Service Analytics

The Self Service option is the basic option available for Twitter Ads. This option is activated for companies with budgets less than $5,000 USD. As a result, the number of analytical tools is restricted. They are:

- **Dashboard:** Twitter will give you an overview of the statistics for impressions, number of clicks, and click rates for promoted Tweets.

- **Follower Chart:** For promoted accounts, Twitter gives you a breakdown of location and days.

Twitter Full Service Analytics

The Full Service option is given to clients who have a budget greater than $5,000 USD. This gives them access to a higher number of analytical tools:

- **Timeline:** This gives you detailed information on your entire advertisement activity.

- **Followers:** This helps you understand how your advertisements are functioning as per the demographics selected.

- **Website Data:** Twitter shows you, in real time, which Tweets and users are the most influential when it comes to traffic to your Website.

- **Download the Data:** Twitter allows you to download all your data in .Csv format and analyze it for a better performance.

■■■

As you can see, Twitter simply cannot be ignored as a platform to grow your business. The level of advertisements, the number of active users, and the functionality puts it at the top of your must-haves for social media platforms for businesses. However, always remember that Twitter will have to approve your business profile first in order for you to use it.

Chapter 27

Google+ Techniques

What is the most visited Website? Google. What is the second most visited Website? YouTube. Get it? Google+ is important and helps with search rankings.

Google+ is the latest social networking platform launched by Google. This service combines all the services offered by Google, such as Gmail and the Google search engine, and allows users to create an integrated community or network of people using Google and its products. As a result, it has become an important networking tool for companies and services. Before we explore its potential, let's look at how we can set up a Google+ accountyou're your business and brand.

How to Set Up a Google+ Account

1. Start by logging into *www.google.com*.

2. Next, click on **Sign In** and log in to your Gmail account. This will bring you back to the main page. However, you will be able to see a plus sign (+) next to your name on the top left-hand side of the page. This is your personal page.

3. Scroll down to the end of the page and click on the option **Business Solutions**. Once you click on this option, you will be directed to the Explore page.

4. Next, click on **Explore Google+ Pages**.

5. Click on **Create a Google (+) Page**. (You will have to do this twice.)

6. There is now a three-step process to complete your page. The first step is to choose the nature of business. Select the option you want and click **Next**.

7. This takes us to step two, **Add Info**. Add your company's name and Website.

8. Next, decide who can see your page.

9. Click on the box next to "I agree to the Pages Terms and I am authorized to create this page" and then click on **Continue**.

10. Here, on the final part of the setup page, you can update your logo and cover page, and add a small description and all your contact information. Click **Finish** to access your page. (Tip: You can add your e-mail, phone number, mobile number, chat ID's (Yahoo, AIM, ICQ, MSN, SKYPE, GTALK, and so on), your physical address, and fax number all at once. To add more contact details, click **Tab** and select the type of contact information to be added.

Here are some final pointers on creating your new page.

▶ Click on the bell icon to switch between your personal and professional pages.

▶ Click on the header **Posts** to share information on your page.

▶ Click on the **About** tab to edit any information about your company or brand.

This completes your setup process!

Adding Content to Your Google+ Account

Your Google+ page depends completely on the content posted by you. While YouTube focuses on the visual aspect, Google+ acts as an all-in-one platform that combines text, images, and videos. Here's how to add content to your Google+ account.

Google+ posts

1. To start with, click on the header called **Posts**. This will bring you to the **Circles** page. If you pay close attention, you will notice that this is similar to a Facebook post.

2. Add text by clicking on the pencil icon, and start typing in the text box.

3. As you can with a Facebook post, you can select the groups you want to share your post with. The default option is always public. To add more groups, click on the plus (+) sign before **Add More People**.

4. To remove a group, please click on the X sign next to that group name.

There are a number of other options provided. These options are:

- **Photos:** You can add any photos specifically related to the post.
- **Video:** You can add a video specific to the material posted.
- **Link:** You can add a link to your Website.
- **Event:** You can generate publicity for a promotional event.

Photos and Videos

As we stated earlier, Google+ is an all-inclusive platform. Hence, it allows you the option of adding photos and videos to your Google+ page.

Photos

Google+ allows you to upload photos and create an album. This album can be shared with people to promote your brand. Click on **Upload New Photos** to upload a photo and add a caption. Click on **Done** and the photo will be uploaded.

Videos

Similarly, Google+ also allows you to create videos and share it on your page. All you have to do is click on **Upload New Videos** to create an album. (Tip: You can add keywords related to your product in your posts as well as captions for your photos and videos.)

Google+ Groups

One of the most important aspects of Google+ is the grouping system. The grouping system is as follows:

- **Everyone:** This includes everybody in your contact list.
- **Following:** This includes only those people whose posts you are following.
- **Customers:** This includes people who have been classified as customers by you.

- **VIPs:** This includes people who have been classified as VIPs by you.

- **Team Members:** This includes people who have been classified as team members by you.

So the question is, how do you classify people? The main point to remember is that only people in your Gmail address book can be classified. To start adding people to any of the previous groups, keep your mouse over the g+ icon.

1. Click on the **People** option. On the top right-hand corner of the page is an option called **Type a Name**. Enter a name, select the individual, and add him or her to any of the groups.

2. If you want to create a new group, click on the circle with the plus (+) icon.

By organizing your contacts into groups, you can control what information is shared with each group much more easily.

How to Advertise On Google+

Now that we have seen how to add content and create groups, let's go over the advertising process. Because we are using a Google product, the main method for advertising is Google Ad words.

1. Start by logging into *Adwords.gogole.com*. Click on the **Sign In** option.

2. Scroll down and click on **+ New Campaign**.

3. You'll have three options to select from: **Search and Display Networks**, **Search Networks Only,** and **Display Networks Only**. The **Search Networks Only** option uses only Google's search engine to reach out to customers, whereas the **Display Networks Only** uses Websites partnered with Google to advertise.

4. Select the first option, the one that uses both networks, and hit **Continue**. This will create a new campaign.

Set up campaign parameters

Let's go through setting up your campaign, step by step. Our first step begins with the General Parameters.

1. Begin by naming your campaign.

2. Next, select if you want a **Standard** campaign or **All Features** campaign. In the **Standard** option, you only have text advertisements that focus on keywords and basic search features. The **All Features** option gives you access to the full power of Google Ads.

3. The next option is **Networks** and **Mobile Devices**. Here you can choose to include or exclude search parameters in Google's search engine. Google Ads will be shown on all computing devices by default.

4. Our next options are **Location** and **Language**. You can select the countries and the cities you want to target. All advertisements will be shown in English. AdWords always selects the first option by default. (Tip: Unless you know how all these options work, please go with the recommended options.)

5. The next options are **Bidding**, **Budget,** and **Delivery**. AdWords always selects the second option by default. You will have to add your daily budget as per your requirement.

6. Next, you need to decide on the delivery method. There are two methods available: the **Standard** method shows the advertisement evenly, which helps preserve your budget for a longer time; and the **Accelerated** method starts displaying your advertisements as quickly as possible. This can be used if you want faster results.

To understand all of these options better, visit: *https://support.google. com/adwords/answer/2375499?hl=en&ctx=cmconstr*

Our final set of options are the advanced settings:

1. First, set up your start and end date.

2. Second, decide on the delivery options for the advertisement. Again, the program selects the ideal optimization features. You can set a limit on the number of impressions.

3. The third option involves your social network settings. The **+1** is an indicator of a Google+ advertisement.

4. The fourth option involves your keywords. You can decide if you want an exact match or a variation match.

5. The final option is called **Dynamic URL**. You can ignore this option.

6. Click on **Save and Continue**.

Set up your advertisement group

This brings us to the next step of the advertisement setup. This is called the **Ad Group**.

1. Start by naming the Ad Group and selecting the type of advertisement.

2. You can select **Text**, **Image**, **Product Listing**, **Dynamic Search**, or **Mobile** advertisements. You can also use an ad builder to build your advertisement. You will be able to see a preview of your ad on the right-hand side of your screen.

3. Next, add keywords related to your product. You can add around 10 to 20 keywords for your advertisement.

4. Next, add the placement options for your advertisement. (Tip: If you leave it blank, the Google network will do the placement on its own.)

5. Once you click **Save and Create Ad Group**, you will be directed to a page that will show you how each keyword will perform.

Now you need to create your bid strategy and budget:

1. Select all options and click on the header **Bid Strategy**.

2. Click on **Choose a Bid Strategy**. This will give you the Flexible Strategy page.

3. Next, click on **Create Flexible Bid Strategy**.

4. On the next page, click **New Bid Strategy**. You can decide if you want more conversions (CPC or CPA), more views (Search Page), or greater number of people clicking on your advertisement (Clicks). Select the strategy and name it.

5. Click on **Save**. This will save the strategy in your campaign.

Now for your budget:

1. On the left-hand side is an option called **Budget**. Click on that and you will be directed to the Budget page.

2. Click on **New Budget** for your budget options.

3. Enter the name, select the campaign, and enter the budget amount (has to be similar to the campaign amount per day) and the delivery method.

4. Click on **Save**.

5. Once you have finished deciding your budget, click on the **Billing** header.

6. AdWords will use your previously saved credit card information to bill you and create your advertisement.

Note that it will take 24 hours before your advertisement is up and running.

An Overview of Your Ad's Performance

Google+ uses Google AdWords to show you how your advertisement is performing. It will also indicate potential factors such as "low traffic keywords." The Google AdWords dashboard can be used to generate a proper report of your advertisement's actual performance.

■■■

As you can see, Google+ harnesses the entire power of Google to make your advertisements extremely powerful. This is the main reason behind the popularity of the business pages in Google+.

Chapter 28
Social Media Tools

Now that you've learned how to use Facebook, LinkedIn, Twitter, YouTube, and Google+ for your business, let's explore a few other social media tools available in the market today.

1. Alterian, or SDL

Formerly known as Alterian, this product is an all-in-one platform. It combines marketing, managing your campaign, and analytics as well as tracking various social media Websites under one all-inclusive roof. You can check out more information here: *www.sdl.com*.

2. Argyle Social

This tool allows you to track potential customers, improve your lead management, and improve existing relationships. This is achieved by combining existing marketing software with social media Websites. Go to *www.argylesocial.com* for more information.

3. Back Tweets

This tool allows you to track followers and people who looked at your Tweets. You can analyze their comments and also search through Twitter for all Websites whose links were populated through Twitter. Check out *www.backtweets.com* for more information.

4. Blitz Metrics

This tool allows you to create social media dashboard across different Websites, such as Twitter and Facebook. You can measure your performance against the competition and also look at which demographic is performing best in which Website. Visit the Website *www.blitzmetrics.com*.

5. Bottle Nose

This tool gives you real-time data for all your social media. The tool combines your activity across all the major social media platforms. You can analyze, monitor, engage, and target your customers from one consolidated real-time tool. Visit the Website *www.bottlenose.com*.

6. Brand Watch

This tool can be used to analyze and then summarize all the content and discussions on your brand(s) as well as those of others. You can add keywords to monitor topics, products, and brands. The tool shows you trends and detailed campaign analysis as well as how your competitors are doing. Visit *www.brandwatch.com* for more information.

7. Buffer

This tool allows you to manage your LinkedIn, Facebook, and Twitter accounts simultaneously. You can schedule updates for each account and get a detailed analysis for all your content. Go to *www.bufferapp.com* for more details.

8. Buzz Equity

This is another tool that monitors your social media activity in real time. You can monitor all your accounts at the same time and check out what consumers are saying about your posts. Visit *www.buzzequity.com* for more details.

9. Carma

This tool allows you to analyze your social media performance based on message penetration and brand recognition. This helps you know which strategies are working well and which need to be revised. You can use this tool to better your sales strategy. Go to *www.carma.com* for more details.

10. Hoot Suite

This is a comprehensive social platform system. It provides users with a single combined dashboard that allows you to manage your workflow, create customized reports, and analyze demographic performance. You can visit *www.hootsuite.com* for more details.

11. Crimson Hexagon

This tool provides you detailed analysis of your social media performance. The tool looks at comments posted by users over different social platforms and then gives you an analysis of how you are performing against the competition. Check out *www.crimsonhexagon.com* for more information.

12. Collective Intellect

This platform is owned by Oracle. It looks at posts across various social networks, including Twitter and Facebook, and analyzes your performance. It looks at customer preferences and their discussions on your brand, and shows the information in real time. Visit *www.collectiveintellect. com* for more information.

13. Social Mention

This tool allows you to search and analyze social media content in real time. The tool captures comments from YouTube, Facebook, and Twitter and displays them in an integrated dashboard. Visit *www.socialmention. com* for more information.

14. Social Response

This tool gives you the capabilities to create more dynamic social media interactions. Using this tool, you can interact with your fans and your consumers on Facebook and Twitter in real time.

15. Sprout Social

This is a Web-based application that allows you to monitor social media pages simultaneously. You can check your performance, generate leads, analyze data, and get competition analysis. You can go to *www. sproutsocial.com* for more information.

16. Fliptop

This platform analyzes a variety of information, including that from social Websites, to provide you access to potential customers, get insights into existing customers, and modify your content to get better results. Website: *www.fliptop.com*.

17. Tweet Beep

This application is an alert function for your Twitter account. You can add keywords and get daily results through your e-mail. Website: *www. tweetbeep.com*.

18. Twitalyzer

This application analyzes your Twitter activity. It looks at items such as followers, mentions, re-Tweets, influencers, and locations. It then provides a one-click analysis of your performance and does a competitive analysis. Go to *www.twitalyzer.com* for more information.

19. Paid Social Media Followers and Likes

There are many companies that will offer you paid fans and followers for Facebook and Twitter. You can find these companies all over the Web. Most of these companies offer a guaranteed number of followers or Likes for your social media page. As tempting as this sounds, the best way to build brand ambassadors (brand ambassadors are customers who not only love your product/service but actively share their experiences with others in their lives and social networks) and awareness is through authentic engagement. Paying for fans and followers is a waste of time and money because Facebook and Twitter regularly remove fake fans and followers. More importantly, the goal in building your social media platform is to increase the likelihood of your followers sharing your message. I have steadily grown my Twitter followers by authentic engagement, which means I continually and consistently interact with followers. In addition, I consistently share my message in a timely manner. Here's an example, I recently flew to the west coast for a client and I had an amazing experience with AirTran Airways. I Tweeted AirTran to let them know how happy I was with my experience. Within two hours, AirTran had responded and thanked me for the feedback. Now *that* is authentic engagement—Gary Vaynerchuk would be proud!

■■■

As you can see, the world of social media offers you a wide variety of tools for your business. However, these are by no means the only tools available. Whether you are new to the social media game or an old pro, *always do your research*. Before using any tool or service, do your due diligence. Look for positive and negative feedback. Also, look for case studies related to these tools. And, *don't assume that paid is better*. The common misconception is that free tools are less effective than the paid ones. However, this is far from the truth. Compare each tool against your requirements and then decide which one fits best.

Chapter 29

Social Media Marketing Techniques

Here are some social media techniques that I have used to build my own audience and followers. I personally enjoy Tweeting and interacting with fans, friends, and followers. People tend to appreciate the time I have taken to engage and share useful information.

Videos, YouTube, and Google Hangout

Use videos to build your authority and provide prospective clients and customers with valuable content. YouTube is the second largest search engine and it's free to use. Here are some tips that will help you create videos that will market your business:

▶ Interview others in your field.

▶ Interview customers/clients.

▶ Take the current news of the day and apply it to your business by offering solutions (job search, refinancing your house, etc.).

▶ Create high-quality videos. For example, it is important to make sure you have enough lighting. Regular lights will not work as well as video lights. You can find good video lighting at B&H or Amazon.com.

▶ The sound in your videos must be top-notch, too. You can use a simple $250 camera from BestBuy. I have shot the majority of my videos using a Kodak Zi8 Camera that I bought for $130. Make sure the camera has a MIC input jack. You can use an external microphone, which will pick up clear and crisp sound. You can find a lavalier, or tie clip microphone, at Radio Shack for less than $30.

▶ Memorizing a script can be difficult so I often use free teleprompter programs such as Teleprompter.com.

Twitter

▶ Follow other Twitter members that are in your industry. For example, you should follow other PR professional if you are in the PR industry.

▶ Create a Twitter list of the people in your industry that you follow. In Twitter, you can create and add people to lists.

▶ Do a Twitter search using keywords from your industry several times a week. Follow the people who come up in the search results. This may appear counterintuitive because you are trying to build a following, but the reality is that connecting with new people in the industry allows you to leverage their networks of followers, networks that you otherwise would not have had access to.

Facebook

■ **Pictures/Infographics:** Page rank in Facebook and studies show that people respond better to visuals than to just text. It is not about you but what information are you sharing with your audience.

■ **Frequency:** Post experiences and information regularly. Facebook has a news feed operation, so posting frequently increases the chances that friends will see your posts and updates.

■ **Consistency:** It is important to be consistent in your message. Try to keep personal information, rants, and potentially inappropriate conversations to a minimum. Regardless of your privacy settings, your pictures and posts are owned by Facebook. Do you really want to leave your future in the hands of someone else? Do not post while you are drunk or in a compromising situation (define that as you will!).

Chapter 30
E-mail Marketing

I recently met with a technology business associate who said, "E-mail marketing is dead!" I have said that traditional advertising and marketing are dead, but I am not that quick to agree about e-mail marketing. The key to e-mail marketing is to present valuable information and content to your niche. I look forward to receiving e-mails from Ramit Sethi, Neil Patel, Derek Halpern, and Brendon Burchard because the content they send me is of extreme value to me. E-mail marketing may be dead as a method of mass marketing and spam, but it is the best way to connect with potential customers that want the value you offer. The importance of targeting your small niche is evident here because potential customers want the content and information you provide. Frequency of the e-mails is not as important as the quality. Your current and potential customers will welcome your e-mails when they recognize you as an authority or expert in your field. So how do you get the e-mails of potential customers?

Simply ask visitors for their e-mail addresses on your Website. On his behavioral economics–based online marketing Website, Socialtriggers.com, Derek Halpern believes you should ask visitors at least three times. He does this by placing opt-in boxes at the top of his blog post, to the right of the blog post, and at the end of the blog post, in addition to a clear call to action: "Sign up for updates" or "Don't miss out on these free updates!"

In addition to offering opt-in boxes on your Website and landing pages, your e-mails to customers must be well-written and valuable. "Well-written" does not mean you have to be a Pulitzer Prize–winning writer, but it does mean that you have to be clear and poignant. To craft a well-written e-mail, ask yourself the following questions:

- What are you trying to tell your customers?
- What do you want them to know?

- Why do they need to read your e-mail?

- What do you want them to do after reading the e-mail?

E-mail Marketing Software

E-mail marketing software offers the ability to schedule, send, and analyze the responses to target e-mails to recipients. You can send e-mails to a large group without having to send one separately to current and potential customers. In addition, the software offers e-mail templates and easy-to-use interfaces to create your messages. There are several options available from a variety of companies that range from free to very expensive. They are:

- **Constant Contact:** Cost range from $15/month to $75/month based on the number of e-mails sent.

- **Mail Chimp:** Costs range from Free to $240/month based on the number of e-mails sent.

- **Aweber:** Costs range from $19/month to $149/month based on the number of e-mails sent.

Here are some important tips for your e-mail marketing campaign that I have used to great effect for my own business:

▶ Make it easy to subscribe: A first name and e-mail address should be the basic info you ask for. Anything more is too much and tends to put people off. Anything less and you will not be able to personalize the e-mail.

▶ Have visitors confirm their e-mail address: Your e-mail marketing software will easily do this for you. More importantly, the e-mails you receive are important for your business; fake e-mails are useless and a waste of time.

▶ Make sure people know what to expect: Tell your audience what they should expect from your e-mails. For example, let them know the type of e-mails they will receive, and the frequency with which they will receive them.

▶ Make sure your e-mails are scannable: I tend to scan e-mails instead of reading them, especially when I am reading them on my tablet or mobile phone. What I scan will dictate whether I invest the time to read it further. You can make it scannable by using shorter paragraphs and bullet lists of important information.

- ▶ Make sure your e-mails are mobile friendly: More people are reading e-mail via their handheld mobile devices. Make it easier for them to become engaged with your content.

- ▶ Test your e-mail results: President Obama did an amazing job with his grassroots e-mail marketing campaign for the 2012 Presidential election. His team meticulously tested every e-mail transmission to determine what worked, when it worked, and why. You should do the same by writing two to three versions of an e-mail and then track the results of each.

- ▶ Make sure to review your analytics: E-mail marketing software offers free analytics or statistics such as: a) open rates, b) click rates, c) the time your e-mails are opened, and d) the number of unsubscribed people.

Resources

Books you need to read:

Dr. Robert Cialdini: *Influence: The Psychology of Persuasion*

Gary Vaynerchuk: *Jab, Jab, Jab, Right Hook: How to Tell Your Story in a Noisy, Social World*

James Altucher and Dick Costolo: *Choose Yourself!*

Grant Cardone: *Sell or Be Sold: How to Get Your Way in Business and in Life*; and *The 10X Rule*

Brendon Burchard: *The Millionaire Messenger*

Blogs you need to read:

Brian Clark—*Copyblogger.com*

Derek Halpern—*Socialtriggers.com*

Neil Patel—*Quicksprout.com*

Ramit Sethi—*Iwillteachyoutoberich.com*

Tim Ferriss—*Fourhourworkweek.com/blog*

Matt Paxton—*5decisionsaway.com*

Paul C. Brunson—*Paulcbrunson.com*

Yanik Silver—*Yaniksilver.com*

Websites you need to visit:

Launcharrow.com for interviews, videos, and training courses to help you grow your business

Ebongeka.com for more on me, my products, and my services.

Appendix

Start-Up Checklist

Structure

□ 1. What's your idea?

□ 2. What problem do you solve?

□ 3. Write an elevator pitch.

□ 4. File your business entity (on Corpnet.com or Legalzoom.com).

Strategy

□ 1. Pricing strategy—do a competition pricing study.

□ 2. Determine your prices.

□ 3. Know your numbers—cost of product/service.

□ 4. Raise your prices incrementally.

Systems

□ 1. Create a process of repeatable tasks.

□ 2. How do you deliver products/services to customer?

□ 3. Search for help—use interns and Vas (virtual assistants).

□ 4. Secure loans if necessary.

□ 5. Build your Website.

Sales

□ 1. Get your first customer.

□ 2. Brush up on social media marketing.

□ 3. Become adept at content marketing.

□ 4. Get out there and start blogging!

Index

A

advertisements, newspaper, 155

angel investors, 131-133

Apple, the startup of, 52

assistants, virtual, 111-112

attorneys, 76

audit triggers, potential, 76-77

authority, sales and, 138

B

bank loans, 130

banners and hoardings, 155

bigger picture, seeing the, 38-39

blogging, importance of, 156

branding, poor, 34-35

business confidence, first
    customers and, 143-144

business idea, complicated, 32

business plan, making a, 19-23

C

capital and money, first
    customers and, 143

capital requirements, fewer, 49

capital, working, 102

commitment, sales, 137

competition pricing, 80-81

consistency, sales, 137

Content Harmony Agency,
    108-109

content management software, 114

content marketing, 147-154

content, Website, 116-117

cost-plus pricing, 83-85

CPA, 75-76

culture, leaders and, 107

customer
  acquisition, lack of, 35
  benefits, elevator pitch and, 62
  service, providing good, 129

customer/market fit, 103-105

D

design, Website, 114-115

donating money, 129

doubts, starting a business with, 9-26

E

economies of scale, 81-83

elements of a Website, 114-115

elevator pitch, 61-64

e-mail marketing, 208-211

employees as partners, 107

enrolled agents, 76

entity
  comparison chart, 69
  structure, 65-72

entrepreneurship, 23

environment, tapping into your immediate, 145

established brands, 46

expenses, marking, 102

expensive prices, good quality and, 139-140

F

Facebook as a platform, 157

Facebook, 27, 159-166
  feedback on, 103
  marketing and, 207
  the growing success of, 13-14
  the startup of, 51
  wasting time on, 147

family, relying on opinions from, 14-16

fears, starting a business and, 9-26

feedback, importance of, 59

first customer, getting your first, 141-145

flyers, 155

for-profit endeavors, 73-74

framing, 135

free Website solutions, 117-126

friends, relying on opinions from, 14-16

Friendster, 27
  failure of, 13

G

Gavankar, Sonya, 54-56

Google, 27
  the startup of, 51

Google+, 195-202

gross profit, 102

H

heuristics, 135

hierarchy model, 45-48

I

idea hierarchy model, 45-48

idea validation, 39
    first customers and, 144-145

idea,
    complicated business, 32
    evaluating your, 37-38
    pursuing your, 11
    premature, 47-48
    recurring, 47
    three main points for
      successful, 38
    useless, 47-48

identifying unique problems, 89

increased pricing, 50

innovation vs. invention, 27-29

interns, 111-112

invention vs. innovation, 27-29

IRS audits, 75

K

keywords, your business and
    Internet, 156

L

leaders, culture and, 107

legal entity, forming a, 70-72

Limited Liability Company, 65-66

limited liability, 66

LinkedIn as a platform, 157

LinkedIn, 167-174
    feedback on, 104

luck, starting a business and, 19

M

market
    inefficiencies, 135
    research, 49

marketing expenses, 102

marketing,
    e-mail, 208-211
    poor, 34-35

mentorship, finding the right, 15

money and capital, first customers
    and, 143

money, raising, 127-133

MySpace, 13, 27

N

newspaper advertisements, 155

niche ideas, 45-46

niche,
    becoming an expert in your,
      53-60
    determining your, 103
    finding your, 49-52
    how to find your, 59-60

novelty items, 47

numbers, knowing your, 101-102

O

opportunity, elevator pitch and, 62

P

pain point, 38-39, 41-43

pamphlets, 155

partnership, 68

partnerships, poorly constructed, 24

pass-through taxation, 66

Pay Per Click, 157

persuasion, the science of, 153-154

pitfalls, small business, 31-35

premature ideas, 47-48

premium Website solutions, 117-126

price, never competing on, 87-91

prices, importance of raising, 59

pricing,
> competition, 80-81
> cost-plus, 83-85
> determining your, 91-97
> increased, 50
> value, 85-87

productivity, sluggish, 24

products, pricing, 91-92

profit margin, 102

profit, gross, 102

R

raising prices, importance of, 59

ranking, businesses and, 156

reciprocation, sales, 136-137

recurring ideas, 47

revenue model, poor, 32-34

revenues, 102

S

sales systems, inadequate, 24

sales, 135-140

scarcity of a product, sales and, 139

S-corporations, 66-67

search engine optimization, 156

services, pricing, 92-97

Silver, Yanik, 58-59

small business pitfalls, 31-35

small business, process for, 108

social media
> marketing techniques, 207-208
> marketing tips, 155-157
> tools, 203-206

social proof, sales and, 137

sole proprietorship, 68

solutions, providing, 89

story, establishing your, 89

storytelling, 147-154

strategy, 79-100

structure, 37-39

Systems, your business and, 105-109

T

tax issues, 73-77

testimonials, importance of, 59

time, starting a business and
> finding, 16-18

timing, elevator pitch and, 63-64

tools, social media, 203-206

traffic, Website, 156

Twitter as a platform, 157

Twitter, 185-194
> feedback on, 103

marketing and, 207

wasting time on, 147

U

unique ideas, importance of, 11-14

useless ideas, 47-48

V

validation, idea, 39

value pricing, 85-87

venture capital, 131-133

ventures, poorly constructed, 24

virtual assistants, 111-112

W

Website traffic, 156

Websites, 113-126

Weebly, creating a website with, 121-126

Wix, creating a Website with, 117-121

working capital, 102

worth, what is your business, 97-100

Y

YouTube as a platform, 157

YouTube, 175-183

feedback on, 104

marketing and, 207

Z

zero-sum game, 27-28

About the Author

EBONG EKA is no stranger to the world of personal finance and lifestyle. As a certified public accountant, former professional basketball player (in Europe), and one of Washington DC's Best-Dressed Men, he offers a fresh perspective in a commanding yet approachable manner that draws a diverse audience. Ebong gives real-life, practical money solutions that are tailored to the average person, the aspiring entrepreneur, and the small-business owner.

Ebong gained experience with some of the largest consulting firms, including PricewaterhouseCoopers and Deloitte & Touche. Ebong is also a tax consulting professional with Levyti Consulting, LLC, a tax advisory firm in the Washington, DC area, and a small-business expert who regularly appears on MSNBC, Fox News, Fox Business Channel, NBC, and CNN. Ebong was also a popular face in primetime and cable television for his role on Bravo's *The Real Housewives of DC*.

For more on Ebong, visit Startmeupbook.com.

Dedication

A very wise person said to me "no book ever comes to fruition in a vacuum." So I dedicate this book to God for keeping His promise to help me through anything.

Acknowledgments

First I must thank my mother, Agatha, for never giving up on us and teaching us the importance of prayer. Thanks also to Umo, Ima, James, Antoine, and the Bradshaws. Also, Matt Paxton, Paul C. Brunson, Fr. James Wells, James Quist, Dr. Marshall Ellens, Laura Wood of FinePrint, the people I've met throughout this journey whose dreams of success have inspired me, and, finally, the fine people at Career Press, Inc., for their belief in this project.